ALL THE COMMANDMENTS OF GOD

—*Volume II*

Hidden Treasures from the Books of Galatians, Ephesians, Philippians and Colossians

Unlock the Mystery to Inherit All the Blessings of God in Your Life

DR. ESTHER V. SHEKHER

WESTBOW
PRESS®
A DIVISION OF THOMAS NELSON
& ZONDERVAN

WestBow Press books may be ordered through booksellers or by contacting:
WestBow Press
A Division of Thomas Nelson & Zondervan
1663 Liberty Drive
Bloomington, IN 47403
www.westbowpress.com
1 (866) 928-1240

Unless otherwise noted, all Scripture quotations in this publication are from the New King James Version of the Bible.

Scripture quotations noted KJV are taken from the Holy Bible, King James Version.

Scripture quotations noted NIV are taken from the Holy Bible, New International Version.

Our Contact Address:
Christ Rules
P.O. Box 994, Galt, CA—95632, USA
Phone: Dr. Esther: 001-626-450-5973
Michelle: 001-480-251-1979
Darla: 001-209-401-1696
Email: christrulesnations@gmail.com
Website: www.christrulesnations.org
Facebook: Christ Rules Nations

ISBN: 978-1-4908-3878-6 (sc)
Library of Congress Control Number: 2014909637

Print information available on the last page.

WestBow Press rev. date: 1/15/2016

"If You Love Me, Keep My Commandments"—Jesus Christ

(Jn.14:15)

This Book is dedicated

To my Beloved Savior and Lord Jesus Christ

Who has given me the Free Gift of Eternal Life.

And Christ Rules My Heart.

Christ Must Rule Our Hearts

Christ Must Rule Our Lives

Christ Must Rule Our Cities

Christ Must Rule Our Nations

For Christ Rules Our Universe.

Contents

Part IV Book Of Colossians

Foreword

As a long time television producer and host, I am required to consider hundreds of books each year for my daily Homekeepers program. No one has ever made the profound impact on my own life like Dr. Esther V. Shekher and her books, ALL THE COMMANDMENTS OF GOD, Volumes 1 and 2. The first time I looked through them, I realized that she has highlighted an important "truth", sorely needed in the church today.

Volume 2 dissects the writings of the Apostle Paul spotlighting the blessings of obedience along with the consequences of disobedience. These books, uniquely formatted, are a refreshing rain in a desert of writings about earthly prosperity and "self" fulfillment. They offer a valuable Biblical resource whether used for personal benefit, a group setting or pulpit series.

Arthelene Rippy
CHRISTIAN TELEVISION NETWORK

Author's Heart

Introduction

I give all praise, glory and honor to our Sovereign God, who, by His grace, has enabled me to finish this second book in the series entitled "All the Commandments of God" which was birthed into my spirit by the Lord God Almighty.

It is my desire that I place this unique book, which reveals the **hidden treasures of God's Word,** in your hands as soon as possible. Against all odds, the Holy Spirit of God has enabled me to highlight all the Commandments of God from the Epistles of Apostle Paul in this divinely directed book.

The commandments are the desires of God's heart; His instructions for us to live a pleasing life before Him. Whenever an instruction of the Lord is followed by rewards or consequences and sometimes both, it is a command. Sometimes they are just direct commandments from the Lord without any rewards or consequences following and we must obey them just because the Lord said so. There is nothing more important than obeying the commandments of God.

Purpose of the Book

Scripture says, if we diligently obey the voice of the Lord our God, to **observe carefully all His commandments, then the blessings will come upon us** and overtake us. Hence I sought the Lord inquiring, "What are the commandments that we ought to obey to inherit all Your blessings?" After praying much in the Spirit for the past ten years, I received this awesome revelation from the Lord. (see Deut.28:1)

Conclusion

The first book in the series from the Gospels of Matthew and John covers almost all the major topics in Christian faith. I have written this second book for those who long for a **much deeper walk with the Lord**. In this book, I have brought out the commandments, the precious truths of God's Word, His hidden treasures, in the simplest format from the Epistles of Paul to the Galatians, Ephesians, Philippians and Colossians which are applicable to us even today.

For **all Scripture is given by inspiration of God**, and is profitable for doctrine, for reproof, for correction, for instruction in righteousness. (2 Tim.3:16)

Apostle Paul states, *"Join together in following my example,* brothers and sisters." (see Phil.3:17)

And, "Be ye followers of me, even as I also am of Christ." (see 1 Cor.11:1/KJV)

Since Apostle Paul himself exhorts us, saying, "Put it into practice—whatever you have learned, or received or heard from me, or seen in me," some of the commandments, which are exemplary, are taken from Apostle Paul's life and experiences on earth; for the rewards and consequences following the commandments are very clear. When we obey these commandments, we will also receive the blessings, as stated by Apostle Paul. (see Phil. 4:9/NIV)

I am confident that this book will bless you beyond your comprehension, just as it has blessed and enriched me writing it for you.

Acknowledgements

I am so grateful to my wonderful family, Vincent, my husband and Sarah, my daughter for supporting me in my calling. I thank my dear friends Monica and Darla who helped me compile this book.

Special thanks to my loving family members, especially my sister, Kanchi and my niece, Beulin for their help in the ministry. I am also indebted to all those who stood with me in prayer for the release of this book.

PART I

Commandments Of God From The Book Of Galatians

Book Of Galatians

Apostle Paul wrote this epistle to the **Churches of Galatia** in the year A.D. 49. Paul and Barnabas together evangelized and established these churches in the cities of Pisidian Antioch, Iconium, Lystra and Derbe during their *first missionary journey.* (see Gal.1:1-2; Acts 13,14; 22:3)

Paul was a man thoroughly trained in the Law under a great scholar named Gamaliel. (see Acts 22:3)

The main theme of this letter is that we receive Salvation by grace through *faith in Jesus Christ* and not by the works of the law.

*Purpose...*Apostle Paul explains that ceremonial laws, such as circumcision, under the old covenant have nothing to do with Salvation under the new covenant which is only by God's grace in Christ.

In this epistle, Paul also emphasizes that we, the NT believers, receive the *power of the Holy Spirit* to live a victorious life, only by faith in the Lord Jesus Christ and not by the works of the law. (see Gal.3:2-5)

Special features... This letter contains a list of the "Fruit of the Holy Spirit" and also a detailed catalogue of the "Works of the Flesh." (see Gal.5:19-23)

Paul clarifies that the true gospel of Christ involves freedom from sin and also freedom from the ceremonial, sacrificial and civil laws of the Old Testament.

Freedom in Christ involves living by the power of the Holy Spirit and fulfilling the law of Christ.

"Put it into practice - whatever you have learned, or received or heard from me, or seen in me," says Apostle Paul. (see Phil. 4:9/NIV; 2 Tim.3:16)

1. Believe In Jesus & Inherit The Blessings of Abraham

COMMANDMENTS OF GOD FOR US TO OBEY	REWARDS FOR OBEDIENCE/ SUPPORTING SCRIPTURES
1. Be those who are of faith in Jesus Christ. (see Gal.3:7,9,14)	1. For it will be accounted to you for *righteousness*. (see Gal.3:6)
2. Believe God just as Abraham did. (see Gal.3:6)	2. Only those who believe are *children of Abraham*. (see Gal.3:7/NIV)
	3. Those who are of faith are *blessed* along with Abraham, the man of faith. (see Gal.3:9/NIV)
	4. God would *justify the nations* by faith. (see Gal.3:8)
	5. You will receive the *promise of the Spirit* through faith in Jesus Christ. (see Gal.3:14, 22)
	6. You will receive the *inheritance in Christ* which God gave to Abraham by promise. (see Gal.3:18)
	7. You will be *justified by faith* in Christ. (see Gal. 3:24)
	8. You are *all sons of God* through faith in Christ Jesus. (see Gal.3:26)
	9. If you belong to Christ, then you are *Abraham's seed, and heirs* according to the promise. (see Gal.3:29/NIV)

The righteous will live by faith. *(see Gal.3:11/NIV)*

1.1 Blessings of Abraham That You Can Inherit Through Obedience

The Price Abraham had to Pay to Possess the Lord's Blessings:

The Lord had said to Abraham,
Get out of your country (**nation**),
from your people (**race**),
and from your father's house (**family**),
to a land that I will show you. (see Gen. 12:1)

I. *Physical Blessings Abraham Received...*

1. I will make *you* into a great nation. (***Power & Authority***) *(see Gen. 13:14-17)*

2. I will bless *you*. (***Prosperity & Security***) *(see Gen.13:2; 14:23)*

3. I will make *your name* great. (***Honor & Position***) *(see Gen. 14:16-20)*

4. *You* will be a blessing. (***Joy & Satisfaction in life***) *(see Gen.14:16 -21)*

5. I will bless those who bless *you*. (***Many friends & Peace***) *(see Gen.13:5,6)*

6. Whoever curses *you*, I will curse. (***God's curse on enemies.***) *(see Gen.12:17; 14:20)*

II. *Spiritual Blessing Abraham Received...*

7. **All nations** will be blessed through you. (*through the Seed of Abraham, **Jesus Christ***) (see Gal.3:8, 16/NIV)

Abraham left in obedience, as the Lord had told him and he and his seed inherited all the above blessings.

Obedience Brings Blessings...We too can inherit the blessings of Abraham by our obedience and faith in Jesus Christ. (see Gen.12:2-4/NIV)

2. Fulfill The Law Of Christ

Following are the topics covered in this chapter:

- Do Good To All & Reap The Harvest
- Examine Your Own Actions
- Be Not Deceived—God Cannot Be Mocked

The Law of Christ... Christ expects us to carry each other's burdens by helping needy people in times of sickness, sorrow and financial stress. When we do so, we fulfill the law of Christ. It simply means fulfilling the **second great commandment of Christ**, "You shall love your neighbor as yourself." (see Matt.22:39)

Only by God's love that is poured out into our hearts through the Holy Spirit, we will be able to fulfill the law of Christ. (see Rom.5:5)

Examine Your Own Actions... We must continuously examine our own actions and bring them in line with the Word of God and set our priorities right by putting God first in our lives. When we do this, we fulfill the **first great commandment of Christ**, "You shall love the Lord, your God with all your heart, with all your soul, and with all your mind." (see Matt.22:37)

Hence, **fulfilling the law of Christ is obeying the two great commandments of Christ.** (see Matt.22:37-39)

2.1 Do Good To All & Reap The Harvest

COMMANDMENTS OF GOD FOR US TO OBEY	REWARDS FOR OBEDIENCE/ CONSEQUENCES OF DISOBEDIENCE
Do good to a sinner: 1. (i) You who live by the Spirit, gently restore the one who is caught in a sin. (see Gal.6:1/NIV) (ii) But watch yourself. (see Gal.6:1/NIV)	i. Or you also may be tempted. (see Gal.6:1/NIV) ii. If anyone **thinks** himself to be something, when he is nothing, he **deceives himself.** (see Gal.6:3)
Do good to all: 2. Bear one another's burdens. (see Gal.6:2)	In this way, you will **fulfill the law of Christ.** (see Gal.6:2/NIV)
Do good to the family of believers: 3. Do not become weary in doing good. (see Gal.6:9/NIV) 4. Do good to all people, especially to those who belong to the family of believers. (see Gal.6:10/NIV)	For **at the proper time you will reap a harvest** if you do not give up. (see Gal.6:9/NIV)
Do good to the one who teaches you God's Word: 5. Share all good things with your instructor. (see Gal.6:6/NIV)	For you receive instruction in the Word from him. (see Gal.6:6/NIV)

2.2 Be Not Deceived—God Cannot Be Mocked

Examine Your Own Actions

COMMANDMENTS OF GOD FOR US TO OBEY	REWARDS FOR OBEDIENCE/ CONSEQUENCES OF DISOBEDIENCE
1. Test your own actions. (see Gal. 6:4/NIV)	Then you can **take pride in yourself alone,** without comparing yourself to someone else; for each one should carry their own load. (see Gal. 6:4-5/NIV)
2. Do not be deceived. (see Gal.6:7) 3. Do not sow to please your flesh. (see Gal.6:8/NIV) 4. Sow to the Spirit (Holy Spirit). (see Gal.6:8)	i. For God is not mocked. (see Gal.6:7) ii. For whatever a man sows, that he will also reap. (see Gal.6:7) iii. Whoever sows to **please their flesh,** from the flesh will reap **destruction.** (see Gal. 6:8/NIV) iv. But he who **sows to the Spirit** will of the Spirit reap **everlasting life.** (see Gal.6:8)

Pause & Think!

God cannot be mocked... Believers who *consciously* sow to please the sinful nature, the flesh, are guilty of mocking and despising God.

We should not keep on *sinning, believing that God would forgive us over and over again.*

If we *take God's grace in vain*, we will certainly reap destruction and death. (see Gal.6:7; Rom.6:20-23; Heb.6:4-8)

3. Know God Or Rather Be Known By God

COMMANDMENTS OF GOD FOR US TO OBEY	CONSEQUENCES OF DISOBEDIENCE/ SUPPORTING SCRIPTURES
1. Know God or rather be known by God.—Apostle Paul (see Gal. 4:9) 2. Do not turn again to the weak and beggarly elements.—Apostle Paul. (see Gal.4:9) 3. Do not observe special days and months and seasons and years. (see Gal. 4:10/NIV)	Or else… i. You will serve those which **by nature are not gods.** (see Gal. 4:8) ii. You will be **enslaved** by the weak and miserable forces all over again. (see Gal. 4:9/NIV)

Pause & Think!

- *Know God…*You can know God by developing an intimate relationship with Jesus Christ, your Savior and by meditating the Word of God. Make Jesus your best friend by spending time with Him in prayer.

- *Be known by God…*When you walk in the fear of the true and living God, Jesus Christ, and live a life of obedience to Him, then you are known by God. And you should be humble enough to be noticed by God. (see 1 Jn.5:20) E.g. King David was so humble before God that he was known by God as *"the man after God's own heart."* (Acts 13:22)

- *This is what the Lord says*—"Israel's King and Redeemer, the Lord Almighty: I am the first and I am the last; **Apart from Me there is no God.** Who then is like Me? Let him proclaim it.

- *Is there any God besides me?* **No**, there is no other Rock; I know not one." (see Is.44:6-8/NIV)

- *What are not gods by nature?…*Created things such as, **sun, moon, stars, animals, trees, mythological characters, idols** made of silver, gold, wood and stone, etc., are few examples of the things which are not gods by nature and therefore should not be worshipped as God. (see Is.44:6-20)

3.1 Magic Spells & Sorceries Will Not Save You!

Our Redeemer, The LORD of Hosts, The Holy One challenges...

- "Keep on with *your magic spells* and with *your many sorceries* which you have labored at since childhood. Perhaps you will succeed, perhaps you will cause terror. (Is. 47:12)

- *All the counsel you have received has only worn you out!* (Is. 47:13)

- Let your *astrologers* come forward, those *stargazers* who make *predictions month by month,* let them save you from what is coming upon you. (Is. 47:13)

- *Surely they are like stubble,* the *fire will burn them up. They cannot even save them*selves from the power of the flame. (Is. 47:14)

- These are not coals for warmth; this is not a fire to sit by. That is all they are to you. These you have dealt with and labored with since childhood. (Is. 47:14-15)

- All of them *go on in their error;* there is *not one that can save you.*" (Is. 47:15)

3.2 Death—Consequence King Saul Faced When He Consulted A Medium/Psychic

Sin of Consulting a Medium/Psychic...

When King Saul saw the Philistine army, he was **afraid; terror filled his heart.** He inquired of the Lord, but the Lord did not answer him by dreams or Urim or prophets. (see 1 Sam.28:4-6)

Saul then said to his attendants, **"Find me a woman who is a medium,** so I may go and inquire of her. There is one in Endor," they said. So Saul disguised himself and at night he and two men went to the woman. **"Consult a spirit for me," he said, "and bring up for me the one I name."** And she did as he requested. (see 1 Sam.28:7-20)

Judgment of God...

Immediately after this incident, God allowed King **Saul and his three sons to be killed in the war** against the Philistines. (see 1 Sam.31:1-7)

Scripture says, **"Saul died for his unfaithfulness** which he had committed against the Lord, because he did not keep the word of the Lord, and also **because he consulted a medium for guidance.** But he did not inquire of the Lord, therefore He killed him, and turned the kingdom over to David." (see 1 Chr.10:13-14)

King Saul did not truly repent of his sins nor did he humble himself and seek the Lord whole heartedly. He did not wait on the Lord until he heard from Him. God was gracious to King Saul though he had disobeyed God's commandments in the past. But when he took the counsel from the witch, **he crossed the line of God's grace** and the judgment of God came upon him. Very sad!

Lessons to Learn...

Do **not seek the counsel of a medium/psychic.** They cannot help you but may bring the judgment of God upon you.

Abomination to the Lord... All those who practice witchcraft and sorcery, those who call upon the dead, and those who go to a medium are an abomination to the Lord. The Lord your God has **not appointed such for you**. (see Deut.18:10-14)

3.3 To Whom Do You Go For Counsel?

- *God alone has counsel and understanding...*

The Lord God Almighty says, "**I will instruct you** and teach you in the way you should go; **I will counsel you** with My eye upon you. (see Job 12:13; Ps.32:8)

- *My counsel shall stand...*(see Is.46:10)

The Lord's counsel is **immutable and unchangeable.** (see Heb.6:17)
The Lord is wonderful in counsel and **excellent in guidance.** (see Is.28:29)

- *Whom does He counsel?*

God's secret counsel is with the **upright.** So repent of your sins, cry out to God for help and He will answer you. (see Prov.3:32; Ps.121:1-2)

The Holy Spirit, Your Counselor... (see Jn.16:13)

The Spirit of the Lord is the **Spirit of counsel** and might. This Spirit of truth, who lives in you, will guide you into all truth. (see Is.11:2)

God is the one who has the answers to all your problems.
His truth is what will set you free.
Why should you go to the world around you for counsel?

4. No Longer You Live, But Christ Lives In You

*Intimacy with Christ...*Those who have faith in Christ should live their lives in intimate union with their Lord, both in His death and resurrection. (see Rom.6:3-5)

*Our old self crucified with Christ...*As a true believer, you are crucified with Christ on the cross. Sin will no longer have control over you and you no longer live but Christ lives in you. (see Rom.6:6,14; Gal.5:24)

*Walk in newness of life in Christ...*You who have been crucified with Christ, now live with Him in His resurrection. ***Christ's power is available to you to make you an over comer of sin.*** It is through the Holy Spirit that Christ's risen life is continuously operating in you. Those who are united with Christ in His death and resurrection are freed from sin's power to walk in newness of life. (see Jn.14-16; Rom.6:1-12; 8:10-11; Acts1:8)

*Being transformed from glory to glory in the image of Christ...*Jesus simply stated that after we are born again, we should ***daily deny ourselves, take up our cross*** and ***follow Him.*** As believers, when we abide in Christ, we are being transformed into the same image of Christ from glory to glory by the Spirit of the Lord. It took Apostle Paul several years to say, "I have been crucified with Christ; it is no longer I who live, but Christ lives in me." (see Lk.9:23; 2 Cor.3:18; Gal.2:20)

*You are made alive in Christ...*You ***reckon yourselves to be dead indeed to sin*** but alive to God in Christ Jesus our Lord. Once you accept Christ, your mindset must be changed how you perceive sin and eventually you will be able to overcome sin by the power of the Holy Spirit. (see Rom.6:11; Eph.2:5)

Commandments on the following topics will help you die to self and walk in newness of life in Christ.

- How does Christ live in you?
- How to be crucified with Christ?
- How to be dead to sin?
- How to be crucified to the world?
- How to live a New Life?

4.1 How Does Christ Live In You?

COMMANDMENTS OF GOD FOR US TO OBEY	REWARDS FOR OBEDIENCE/ SUPPORTING SCRIPTURES
1. Be crucified with Christ, as apostle Paul was. (see Gal.2:20)	i. Then it is no longer you who live, but *Christ lives in you.* ii. The life which you now live in the flesh, you *live by faith in the Son of God*, who loved you and gave Himself for you. (see Gal.2:20)
2. *Crucify the sinful nature* with its passions and desires. (see Gal.5:24/NIV) 3. Let us not become conceited, provoking and envying each other. (see Gal.5:26/NIV)	For those who *belong to Christ* have crucified the sinful nature with its passions and desires. (see Gal.5:24/NIV)

Points to Ponder:

- *Crucified with Christ...Now if we died with Christ, we will also live with Him.* If we have been united with Christ in His death, we will certainly be united with Him in His resurrection. (see Rom.6:5,8)

  Apostle Paul explains that crucifying your sinful nature is an ongoing process because your spirit which has been crucified and died with Christ, still resides within the flesh which is very much alive. (Rom.7:18-25)

- *The Holy Spirit enables you to crucify the flesh...*You cannot overcome your inherited sinful nature on your own but you need the power and guidance of the Holy Spirit to die to "Self." The Holy Spirit changes you from producing the deeds of the flesh to producing the fruit of the Spirit. (see Rom.8:2)

- *Christ lives in you...*When Christ lives in you, His Power is within you, becoming the source of all of life and the centre of all your thoughts, words and deeds. (see Jn.15:1-6)

- *Live by faith in the Son of God...*Those who put their faith in Christ will live their lives in *intimate union with their Lord Jesus Christ; for Christ is the True God and Eternal Life.* (see 1 Jn.5:20)

4.2 How To Be Crucified With Christ?

COMMANDMENTS OF GOD FOR US TO OBEY	REWARDS FOR OBEDIENCE/ SUPPORTING SCRIPTURES
1. Count yourselves **dead to sin** but alive to God in Christ Jesus. (see Rom.6:11/NIV; Gal.2:20; 5:24)	i. *For sin shall not be your master,* because you are not under law, but *under grace.* (see Rom.6:14/NIV)
2. Do not let sin reign in your mortal body so that you obey its evil desires. (see Rom.6:12/NIV)	ii. *If Christ is in you, the body is dead because of sin,* but the Spirit *is* life because of righteousness. (see Rom.8:10)
3. Do not offer the parts of your body to sin, as instruments of wickedness; but rather offer yourselves to God. (see Rom.6:13/NIV)	iii. For our old man was **crucified with Him,** that the body of sin might be done away with, that **we should no longer be slaves of sin.** (see Rom.6:6)
4. Offer the parts of your body to Christ **as instruments of righteousness**. (see Rom. 6:13/NIV)	iv. For he who has died has been **freed from sin.** (see Rom.6:7)

4.3 How to be Dead to Sin?

It is impossible to be dead to sin except by the Holy Spirit...

- *Through the Holy Spirit...*You cannot be dead to sin in your own strength. But you can overcome your flesh when you totally depend on the power of the Holy Spirit; for the **Lord is that Spirit.** (see 2 Cor.3:17)

  The more the Holy Spirit of God fills you with the glory of God and empowers your inner man, the more you will be dead to sin.

- *Through the Son, Jesus...* If the Son sets you free, you will be free indeed. Through Christ, the Spirit who gives life will set you *free from the law of sin* and death. (see Jn.8:36; Rom.8:2/NIV)

- *By the Fullness of Christ...You should be filled with the fullness of Christ (100 %)* to be dead to sin. (see Eph. 4:13)

- *The extent to which you allow Christ* to live in you, to the *same extent* you will be dead to sin. (see Rom.8:10)

- *How to be filled with the Fullness of Christ?* Know the love of Christ which passes knowledge; so that you may be filled with *all the fullness of God.* (see Eph. 3:17-19; 4:13)

It is a process through which God will take you until you are filled with the fullness of Christ. As you yield to the Spirit of God and *wait on the Lord* in the Most Holy Place, you will be filled with His Glory, i.e., the fullness of Christ.—*From Author's Experience.*

4.4 How To Be Crucified To The World?

You are crucified to the world only through Christ.

COMMANDMENTS OF GOD FOR US TO OBEY	REWARDS FOR OBEDIENCE/ SUPPORTING SCRIPTURES
1. *Never boast except in the Cross* of our Lord Jesus Christ, as apostle Paul stated. (see Gal.6:14/NIV)	i. For *only through Christ, the world is crucified to you* and you to the world, as it was for apostle Paul. (see Gal.6.14) ii. For it is *by grace you have been saved,* through faith—and this not of yourselves, it is the *gift of God—not by works, so that no one can boast.* (see Eph.2:8-9) iii. As many as *walk according to this rule, peace and mercy* be upon them, and *upon the Israel* of God. (see Gal.6:16)
2. Do not subject yourself to the regulations (ways) of the world. (see Col. 2:20/NIV)	i. *For you have died with Christ* to the basic principles of this world. ii. If you submit to the rules of the world, it is as though *you still belong to the world.* (see Col.2:20/NIV)
3. Do not submit to the rules of the world - "Do not handle! Do not taste! Do not touch!" which are based on merely *human commands and teachings.* (see Col. 2:21-22/NIV)	i. For these rules have to do with things that are *all destined to perish with use.* (see Col. 2:22/NIV) ii. For such regulations indeed have an appearance of wisdom, with their self-imposed worship, their false humility and their harsh treatment of the body, but *they lack any value in restraining sensual indulgence.* (see Col. 2:23/NIV)

4.5 How To Live A New Life?

COMMANDMENTS OF GOD FOR US TO OBEY	REWARDS FOR OBEDIENCE/ SUPPORTING SCRIPTURES
1. **Be baptized into Christ's death.** (see Rom. 6:3) 2. **Be buried with Christ** through baptism into His death. (see Rom. 6:4/NIV)	So that, just as Christ was raised from the dead *through the glory of the Father,* **we too may live a new life.** (see Rom.6:4/NIV)
3. Be baptized into Christ. (see Gal.3:27)	For you will **put on Christ.** (see Gal.3:27)

It is **only through the Holy Spirit,** Christ's risen life will manifest in you. (see Jn.16:13-14)

For more details on "How to live a new life", please refer to **chapter 2 in the Book of Ephesians in this book.**

Pause & Think!

In order **to die 100% to sin, flesh & the world,** *a believer should consider himself to be...*

1.   **Crucified with Christ.** (see Gal.2:20)

2.   **Dead with Christ.** (see Col.2:20)

3.   **Baptized into Christ's death.** (see Rom.6:3)

4.   **Buried with Christ** through baptism into His death. (see Rom.6:4)

5.   **United with Christ** in His death. (see Rom.6:5)

6.   **United with Christ in His resurrection.** (see Rom.6:5)

When you are crucified, baptized into Christ's death and buried with Christ, you will be totally dead to sin (100%) and sin will not have dominion over you. (see Rom.6:1-14)

Holy Spirit, Your Helper...You don't need to strive to be crucified with Christ to die to self. But as you yield to the Holy Spirit and remain still in His Presence, you will eventually be transformed into the likeness of Christ.—*From Author's Experience*

Now, if you died with Christ, *you will also live with Him.* (see Rom.6:8)

Then you will be an over-comer and *receive the rewards of an over-comer* in Heaven. (see Rev.2-3)

5. Teachers Of God's Word

Following are the topics covered in this chapter:

- Do not distort the Gospel of Christ
- Do not try to win the approval of men
- Be a Servant of Christ as Apostle Paul was

Do not pervert the Gospel of Christ...Apostle Paul cautions the teachers of God's Word not to turn to a different gospel which is not a gospel at all, but preach the good news only by the revelation of Jesus Christ, as he did.

In these last days, many are distorting the truth of the Gospel of Christ, confusing the innocent and the new believers. Paul warns that if anyone preaches the gospel other than the Gospel of Jesus Christ, **he will be under God's curse.** (see Gal.1:7-12/NIV)

5.1 Do Not Distort The Gospel Of Christ

The Gospel of Christ is the good news of salvation that comes through faith by the grace of Jesus Christ who died in our place, rose again and is still alive.

COMMANDMENTS OF GOD FOR US TO OBEY	CONSEQUENCES OF DISOBEDIENCE
1. Do not turn away from God who called you in the grace of Christ to a different gospel, as apostle Paul says. (see Gal.1:6) 2. Do not pervert the gospel of Christ.—Apostle Paul. (see Gal.1:7) 3. Do not preach the gospel according to man; but *by the revelation of Jesus Christ,* as Apostle Paul did. (see Gal.1:11-12)	*For if anyone or even an angel from heaven should preach a gospel other than the gospel of Christ, let him be **accursed.** (see Gal.1:8-9/NIV)*

5.2 Do Not Try To Win The Approval Of Men

Jesus said to the Pharisees, "You are the ones who justify yourselves in the eyes of men, but God knows your hearts. *For what is highly valued among men is detestable in God's sight.*" (Luke.16:15/NIV)

COMMANDMENTS OF GOD FOR US TO OBEY	CONSEQUENCES OF DISOBEDIENCE
1. Do not persuade men but God. (see Gal.1:10) 2. Do not try to please men, as apostle Paul says. (see Gal.1:10/NIV)	For if you please men, you will *not be a servant of Christ.* (see Gal.1:10/NIV)
3. Do not be highly esteemed among men. (see Luke.16:15)	For it is *an abomination* in the sight of God. (see Luke.16:15)

* *For more commandments on this topic, please read Chapter 26 "Teachers of God's Word" in my first book titled "All the Commandments of God." Volume I.*

5.3 Be A Servant Of God As Apostle Paul Was

Apostle Paul, not a men-pleaser... When Paul had the call directly from the Lord Jesus to preach the gospel among the gentiles, *he did not consult any man,* nor did he go up to Jerusalem to see Peter, James and John who were apostles before him. He did not seek their approval to do the Lord's will for his life. (see Gal.1:16-17)

Apostle Paul was not swayed by people of position and power. For he says, "As for *those who seem to be important - whatever they were, makes no difference to me; God shows personal favoritism to no man.* (see Gal. 2:6/NIV)

Apostle Paul, a man of Prayer... Paul went immediately into Arabia and spent time alone with God. It was a time of preparation for Apostle Paul for the great ministry ahead among the gentiles. (see Gal.1:18)

Apostle Paul, a God-pleaser... After three years in Arabia, Paul went up to Jerusalem to see Peter and stayed with him for fifteen days. *Then after fourteen years only,* he went up again to Jerusalem *by revelation of God* and communicated with Peter and the other disciples about how he ministered among the gentiles and that he had not been running his race in vain. (see Gal.1:18-24; 2:1-2)

Apostle Paul was totally dependent on God for guidance and fulfilled God's perfect will for his life. For he says, "Am I now trying to win the approval of human beings, or of God? *If I were still trying to please people, I would not be a servant of Christ."* (see Gal.1:10/NIV)

Be a God-pleaser and not a men-pleaser... Once you become a believer, you should make all efforts to please only God even if it means displeasing your friends, family members and people of position and power.

6. Unity—You Are All One In Christ Jesus

COMMANDMENTS OF GOD FOR US TO OBEY	REWARDS FOR OBEDIENCE/ SUPPORTING SCRIPTURES
You all be one in Christ Jesus—Apostle Paul. (see Gal.3:28/NIV)	1. For in Christ, there is neither Jew nor Greek, neither *slave* nor free, neither *male nor female.* (see Gal.3:28/NIV)
	2. For as many of you as were baptized into Christ have *put on Christ.* (see Gal.3:27)

Pause & Think!

*Put on Christ...*Apostle Paul states that there are no ethnic, national, linguistic, socio economic and gender barriers *when you have intimate relationship with the Lord Jesus Christ.*

7. Your Spirit In Conflict With The Flesh

Spirit against the flesh… The flesh desires what is contrary to the Spirit and the Spirit desires what is contrary to the sinful nature, the flesh. They are in conflict with each other. (see Gal.5:17/NIV)

Walk by the Spirit and you will not gratify the desires of the flesh. (see Gal.5:16/NIV)

Those who are Christ's have crucified the flesh with its passions and desires. (see Gal.5:24; 5:1/NIV)

COMMANDMENTS OF GOD FOR US TO OBEY	CONSEQUENCES OF DISOBEDIENCE
1. Do not practice the "works of the flesh." (see Gal. 5:19-21)	For those who practice the works of the flesh will **not inherit the Kingdom of God.** (see Gal. 5:19-21)
2. Do not conduct yourselves in the lusts of your flesh, fulfilling the desires of the flesh and of the mind.—Apostle Paul. (see Eph.2:3)	Or else you will be **"children of wrath,** *just as the others."*—Apostle Paul. (see Eph.2:3)

7.1 The Unrighteous Will Not Inherit The Kingdom of God

I. *The Works of The Flesh...*

1. Adultery

2. Fornication

3. Uncleanness

4. Licentiousness (recklessness)

5. Idolatry

6. *Sorcery*

7. *Hatred*

8. *Contentions (strife)*

9. Jealousies

10. Outburst of *wrath*

11. *Selfish ambitions*

12. Dissensions (rebellion)

13. Heresies

14. *Envy*

15. Murders

16. *Drunkenness*

17. Revelries (wild partying) and those who practice such things will *not inherit the kingdom of God.* (see Gal.5:19-21)

II. *Do not be deceived...*

Neither fornicators, *nor adulterers,*
nor homosexuals, nor sodomites,
nor idolaters,
nor thieves, nor extortioners,
nor covetous,
nor drunkards, nor revilers will inherit the kingdom of God. (see 1 Cor.6:9-10)

8. You Are Not Under Law, But Under Grace

Christ has redeemed us from the curse of the law, having become a curse for us; for it is written, "Cursed is everyone who hangs on a tree". (see Gal.3:13)

The word "Law" (Heb. Torah) means "teaching or direction".

Three Divisions of Law…The Law of God given to Moses can be divided into 3 categories:

1. *The moral law* deals with God's standards for holy living. (see Ex.20:1-17)
2. *The civil law* deals with Israel's legal and social life. (see Ex.21–23)
3. *The ceremonial law* deals with the form and ritual of Israel's worship of the Lord, including the sacrificial system. (see Ex.24:12-31:18)

What was the purpose of the law? (see Gal. 3:19)

Is the law against the promises of God? Certainly not! (Gal. 3:21)

The law was added because of transgressions until the Seed, Jesus Christ had come to whom the promise was made. It brings unconscious sin into consciousness and makes people actual transgressors. (see Gal. 3:19)

*Conviction of sin…*The law convicted people of sin until Jesus Christ came but after Christ, the Holy Spirit of God in us convicts us of sin. (see Gal.3:19; Jn.16:8)

8.1 You Are Redeemed From The Law Through Christ

Christ declared "Do not think that I came to destroy the Law or the Prophets. *I did not come to destroy but to fulfill.*

For assuredly, I say to you, till heaven and earth pass away, *one jot or one tittle will by no means pass from the law till all is fulfilled.*" (see Matt.5:17-18)

Jesus fulfilled the sacrificial and ceremonial law at the cross by becoming the Lamb of atonement that was slain once for all, to redeem us from our sins and from the law. (see Gal.3:19; Heb.10:10)

Jesus obeyed the moral law by leading a sinless life on this earth. The moral law, i.e. the commandments of God, which deals with God's standard of righteousness is still applicable to us today. *These laws are not for our salvation* but they will help our spiritual growth. (see Heb.4:15; Ex.20:1-17)

So when Paul says, "You are redeemed from the law," what he means is that *we must not view the law* as a system of legal commandments *for our Salvation.* For salvation comes only through faith in Jesus Christ. (see Rom.10:9)

I. *The Laws that the Believer is Obligated to Keep Include;*

*   The ethical and moral principles of the OT.
*   The teachings of Christ and the Apostles.

These laws reveal God's moral nature and His will for His people and, therefore still apply today. By obeying them, we express the life of Christ in us.

II. *The Laws that No Longer Apply to the Believers:*

The OT Laws that apply directly to the nation of Israel, such as…

- Sacrificial Law (see Lev.1:2-3)
- Ceremonial Law or ritual (e.g., circumcision) (see Heb.10:1-10)
- Social Law relates to Israel's social life.
- Civil Law which deals with Israel's legal system.

COMMANDMENTS OF GOD FOR US TO OBEY	REWARDS FOR OBEDIENCE
Redemption in Jesus:	*For Believers:*
Be redeemed from the law through God's Son, Jesus Christ.—Apostle Paul (see Gal.4:4-5)	1. So that you might receive the **adoption as sons.** (see Gal.4:5)
	2. Because you are sons, God sent the **Spirit of His Son into your hearts**, the Spirit who calls out, Abba, Father. (see Gal.4:6/NIV)
	3. You are **no more a servant**, but a son. (see Gal.4:7/KJV)
	4. Since you are a son, God has made you also **an heir** through Christ. (see Gal.4:7/NIV)

This commandment of God applies to the unbelieving gentiles.

8.2 Why Should We Obey The Old Testament Moral Laws?

- **Commandments, Prophecies & Promises of God…**The moral law i.e., the commandments of God, the prophecies concerning the Second Coming of Christ and the promises of God in the Old Testament, all will be fulfilled even to the jot and tittle till heaven and earth pass away, as Jesus declared. (see Matt.5:17-18)

- Jesus Himself states that **God's commandment is life everlasting.** (see Jn.12:50)

- **If Christ has upgraded** the commandments in the Old Testament then we should obey His upgraded commandments. The commandments which are not upgraded by Jesus will remain as they are and must be obeyed.

- **Obedience to the least of God's Commandments…**Jesus also stated that whoever breaks one of the least of God's commandments, and teaches men so, shall be called least in the kingdom of heaven; but whoever does and teaches them, he shall be called **great in the kingdom of heaven.** (see Matt.5:19)

- **Jesus Counsels the Rich Young Ruler and affirms the need to obey God's Commandments….**

  A rich young ruler came to Jesus and said, "Good Teacher, **what good thing shall I do that I may have eternal life?"**

  Jesus said to him, But **if you want to enter into life, keep the commandments."**

  He said to Him, "Which ones?" Jesus said, "'You shall not murder,' 'You shall not commit adultery,' 'You shall not steal,' 'You shall not bear false witness,' 'Honor your father and *your* mother,' and, 'You shall love your neighbor as yourself.' " (see Matt.19:16-19)

  In Matthew 19:16, Jesus was asked what must be done to inherit eternal life. Jesus then listed several of the Ten Commandments from the Old Testament to the rich young ruler, thereby emphasizing that we need to obey God's commandments.

- *Importance of Obeying the Commandments of God mentioned in the Book of Revelation...*

In Rev.12:17, Satan or the dragon, who deceives the whole world when he was cast to the earth went to make war with those who **keep the commandments of God** and hold to the testimony of *Jesus*.

Again, Rev.14:12 mentions about the patience of the saints who **keep the commandments of God** and the faith of Jesus.

- *You can obey the Commandments of God only by the power of the Holy Spirit...*

In the Old Testament, people obeyed the commandments of God out of fear of judgment.

But in the New Covenant, we obey the commandments out of love for God. After Christ came, the power of the Holy Spirit is available to help us obey the commandments of God. The Holy Spirit working within us empowers us to live a righteous life before God.

8.3 Relying On The Works Of The Law For Our Salvation Brings A Curse

1. *"Is the Law sin? Certainly not...* Indeed I would not have known what sin was except through the Law." For example, "I would not have known what coveting really was if the Law had not said, 'Do not covet.'" (see Rom.7:7)

2. And I found out that my spirit was dead because of my sin. "Therefore **the Law is holy and the commandment holy and just and good.** Was then that which is good made **death unto me?** God forbid!" (see Rom.7:12-13)"

   "We know that the **Law is spiritual** but we are carnal sold under sin." states apostle Paul. (see Rom.7:14)

3. Apostle Paul also says, *I delight in the Law* of God in my inner being. So then, with the mind *I myself serve the law of God,* but with the flesh the law of sin. (see Rom.7:22,25)

4. Hence, we believers should no longer look to the OT Law and sacrifices for our salvation and acceptance from God. Apostle Paul states that *if we look to the law for our salvation, then we are under a curse.*

5. Now that we are united to Christ, we should **look to Christ for our salvation.** Since **Christ has fulfilled the ceremonial and the sacrificial law** at the cross, if we still follow these laws for our salvation, we will be under a curse. (see Gal.3:10)

6. The law is not of faith, but the man who does them (i.e. commandments) *shall live by them.* (see Gal.3:12)

7. Grace and obedience to the moral law, i.e. the commandments of God are not in conflict, for they both point to righteousness and holiness. (see Rom.7:12-13)

COMMANDMENTS OF GOD FOR US TO OBEY	CONSEQUENCES OF DISOBEDIENCE/ SUPPORTING SCRIPTURES
1. Do not rely on the works of the law (*ceremonial & sacrificial law*). (see Gal.3:10/NIV)	1. *For all who rely* on the works of the law are *under a curse.* (see Gal.3:10/NIV)
	2. "*Cursed* is everyone who does not continue to do *everything* written in the Book of the Law." (see Gal.3:10/NIV; Deut. 27:26)
	3. *No one is justified* by the law in the sight of God. (see Gal. 3:11)
	4. The law cannot annul the covenant that was confirmed to Abraham by God in Christ. (see Gal. 3:16-17)
	5. For your inheritance is not of the law but by the promise of God in Christ. (see Gal.3:18)
	6. There is *no law that could impart life.* (see Gal.3:21)
	7. Righteousness does not come by the law. (see Gal.3:21)
2. Die to the law (ceremonial & sacrificial law), as Apostle Paul did. (see Gal.2:19)	So that you might live for God. (see Gal.2:19)

Pause & Think!

- *"Do we then make void the law?"* What does apostle Paul mean by this?

  Apostle Paul states, "Do we then make void the law through faith? *Certainly not! On the contrary, we establish the law."* (see Rom.3:31)

- **We establish the law…**Salvation in Christ does not mean that the law has no value. In fact, justification by faith upholds the law.

- Scripture says, *Without shedding of blood there is no remission of sins.* (see Heb.9:22)

In the Old Testament, animal's blood was shed for the remission of people's sins. But when Jesus died on the Cross, the blood sacrifice was made once for all as atonement for our sins.

Since Christ has fulfilled the sacrificial and the ceremonial laws at the cross, when we make peace with God through the precious blood of Jesus Christ, we establish the law. (see Heb.10:10; Rom.5:1)

8.4 Righteousness, Not By The Works Of The Law

- If a law had been given that could impart life, then righteousness would certainly have come by the law. (see Gal.3:21)

- A man is not justified by the works of the law but by faith in Jesus Christ; for by the works of the law (e.g. circumcision) no flesh shall be justified. (see Gal.2:16)

- The Scripture declares that the whole world is a prisoner of sin. But the *righteousness from God comes through faith in Jesus Christ* to all who believe in Him. (see Gal.3:22; Rom.3:22)

- Christ Jesus becomes for us wisdom from God and *righteousness and sanctification and redemption*. (see 1 Cor.1:30)

COMMANDMENTS OF GOD FOR US TO OBEY	REWARDS FOR OBEDIENCE/ CONSEQUENCES OF DISOBEDIENCE
Grace Of God: 1. Do not set aside the grace of God—Apostle Paul. (see Gal 2.21)	i. For if righteousness comes through the law i.e., by works and not by grace, then **Christ died in vain**. (see Gal.2:21) ii. For it is **by grace you have been saved,** through faith and this not from yourselves, it is the **gift of God** not by works, so that no one can boast. (see Eph.2:8-9/NIV) iii. What then? Shall we sin because we are not under law but under grace? **Certainly not!** (see Rom.6:15-18)
2. Know that a person is not justified by the works of the law.—Apostle Paul. (see Gal.2:16/ NIV)	But a person is **justified only by faith in Jesus Christ.**—Apostle Paul. (see Gal.2:16)
3. Put your faith in Christ Jesus – Apostle Paul. (see Gal.2:16/NIV)	So that you may be **justified by faith in Christ** and not by the works of the law (i.e. circumcision). (see Gal.2:16/NIV) Because by the works of the law no one will be justified. (see Gal.2:16/NIV)

8.5 You Are Not Made Perfect By The Works Of The Law

COMMANDMENTS OF GOD FOR US TO OBEY	CONSEQUENCES OF DISOBEDIENCE/ SUPPORTING SCRIPTURES
To the Backslider: 1. Do not try to be made perfect by the flesh, if you have begun in the Spirit.—Apostle Paul. (see Gal. 3:3; Heb.7:19) 2. Receive the Spirit by the hearing of faith and not by the works of the law.—Apostle Paul. (see Gal. 3:2,5)	i. Or else, you are foolish! ii. You will suffer much for nothing.—Apostle Paul. (see Gal. 3:3-4/NIV) iii. For Christ supplies the Spirit to you and works miracles among you, by the hearing of faith and not by the works of the law. (see Gal.3:5)
3. Do not let anyone bewitch you from obeying the truth (concerning circumcision).—Apostle Paul. (see Gal. 3:1)	i. If you do, then you are *foolish,* as apostle Paul says. ii. For before your very eyes *Jesus Christ was clearly portrayed as crucified.* (see Gal. 3:1/NIV)

Pause & Think!

- After beginning your walk with the Lord in the Holy Spirit, *if you think you can be made perfect by observing the works of the law (e.g., circumcision), then you are foolish* and you will suffer much for nothing, as Apostle Paul said. (see Gal.3:1-4)

- The Lord says to the backsliding believer, "Remember from where you have fallen; repent and do the first works." (see Rev. 2:5)

8.6 The Holy Spirit Makes You Perfect

- *Holy Spirit through Christ, not by works of the law...*We receive the power and the anointing of the Holy Spirit only by believing in Jesus Christ, the Son of God and not by observing the works of the law. *The Holy Spirit of God makes you perfect in the sight of God.* (see Rom.8:2)

- When we rely on the power of the Holy Spirit, He enables us to resist the power of sin. For the *law of the Spirit of life in Christ Jesus sets us free from the law of sin* and death. (see Rom.8:2)

- *Works of the law...*Circumcision, sacrificing animals as sin offering, following traditions, rituals, superstitions, etc., are some examples of the works of the law.

8.7 Sacrificial Law & Grace Cannot Co-Exist

- Apostle Paul states that the law is insufficient to redeem us apart from grace of Jesus Christ. (see Rom.5:21; Gal.3:21)

- What the law could not do, in that it was weak through the flesh, God did by sending His own Son in the likeness of sinful flesh to be a sin offering. (see Rom. 8:3)

- Jesus, by the ransom of His own blood, has redeemed us from the power of sin and therefore sin shall no longer be your master. (see Rom. 6:14/NIV; 8:2)

- In fact, the name *"Jesus" means He will save His people from their sins.* (see Jn. 8:36; Matt.1:21)

COMMANDMENTS OF GOD FOR US TO OBEY	CONSEQUENCES OF DISOBEDIENCE/ SUPPORTING SCRIPTURES
Abraham had two sons; one by the slave woman and the other by the free woman;	For the son of the slave woman shall **not be heir** with the son of the free woman. (see Gal.4:30)
Get rid of the slave woman and her son. (Sacrificial law) (see Gal.4:22,30)	(Similarly, ceremonial, sacrificial law and grace of Christ cannot co-exist.) (see Gal.4:21-31)

Pause & Think!

*Get rid of the sacrificial law...*We, believers are not children of the slave woman but of the free i.e., we do not come under the sacrificial law but under grace of Christ. (see Gal.4:31)

*Jesus Christ, our Sacrificial Lamb...*We don't need to offer animal sacrifices any more as atonement for our sins. For Christ, the Lamb of God has been slain once for all to redeem us from our sins. (see Heb.10:4; Jn.1:29; Eph.1:7)

8.8 Two Covenants—Law & Grace

- *Two sons—Slave and Free*...It is written that Abraham had two sons; one by the slave woman and the other by the free woman. (see Gal.4:22/ NIV)

- *Sons of Flesh and Promise*... Abraham's son by the slave woman was born according to the flesh; but his son by the free woman was born as the result of a promise of God. (see Gal.4:23/NIV)

- *Two Covenants*...These things are symbolic. For *the women represent two covenants*. (see Gal.4:24/NIV)

- *First Covenant—Hagar, the slave woman* ...One covenant is from Mount Sinai and bears children who are to be slaves; this is Hagar. (see Gal.4:24/NIV)

- *Hagar, the earthly Jerusalem*...Now Hagar stands for Mount Sinai in Arabia and corresponds to the present *city of Jerusalem,* because she is *in sin of slavery* with her children. (see Gal.4:25/NIV)

- *Second Covenant—Sarah, The Free Woman*...But the Free woman is symbolic of the city of New Jerusalem in Heaven. (see Gal.4:26/NIV)

- *Sarah, The Free Woman, The New Jerusalem*...The Free woman is symbolic of the city of New Jerusalem in Heaven. (see Gal.4:26/NIV)

- *Believers, The Children of Promise*...Now we, brethren, as Isaac *was,* are children of promise. (Gal.5:28)

So then, we believers are not children of the slave woman but of the free woman, meaning, we no longer come under the ceremonial and sacrificial law but under the grace of Jesus Christ. (see Gal.4:21-31/NIV)

8.9 Freedom In Christ

- *Freedom Through Christ...* If the Son makes you free, you shall be free indeed. It is *for freedom* that Christ has set us free. (see Jn.8:36; Gal.5:1/NIV)

- *Freedom Through The Word of God...* You shall know the truth, and the truth shall make you free. (see Jn.8:32)

- *Freedom Through The Holy Spirit...* **The Lord is the Spirit;** and where the Spirit of the Lord is, there is liberty. For the anointing breaks the yoke of bondage. (see 2 Cor. 3:17-18; Is.10:27)

COMMANDMENTS OF GOD	CONSEQUENCES OF DISOBEDIENCE
1. Stand fast in the liberty by which Christ has made us free. (see Gal.5:1) 2. Be not entangled again with a yoke of bondage. (e.g., circumcision). (see Gal.5:1) 3. Do not be circumcised.—Apostle Paul (see Gal.5:2) 4. Do not let anyone hinder you from obeying the truth (concerning circumcision).—Apostle Paul. (see Gal. 5:7)	Apostle Paul declares that you should be *liberated from the practice of circumcision* which comes under the law. i. If you let yourselves be circumcised, then *Christ will be of no value to you at all*. (see Gal.5:2/NIV) ii. Every man who lets himself be circumcised is *obligated to obey the whole law.* (see Gal.5:3/NIV) iii. You who are trying to be justified by the law have been *alienated from Christ*; you have *fallen away from grace*. (see Gal.5:4/NIV) iv. This persuasion (to do circumcision) *does not come from Him* who calls you. (see Gal. 5:8) v. He who troubles you (in regards to circumcision), *shall bear his judgment*, whoever he is. (see Gal.5:10)

5. Through the Spirit, eagerly wait for the hope of *righteousness by faith* (not by the works of the law e.g., circumcision). (see Gal.5:5)	i. For in Christ Jesus neither circumcision nor uncircumcision avails anything, *but faith* working through love. (see Gal.5:6/NIV)
	ii. In Christ Jesus, neither circumcision nor uncircumcision means anything; *what counts is a new creation.* (see Gal. 6:15/NIV)

Pause & Think!

- Here Apostle Paul was referring to the freedom, especially from the tradition of circumcision, since Christ has made us free.

- *The righteousness of God* comes only by faith in Jesus Christ through the Holy Spirit and not by circumcision which is the work of the law. (see Rom.3:22; Gal.5:5-6/NIV)

8.10 Do Not Abuse Your Freedom In Christ But Love One Another

COMMANDMENTS OF GOD FOR US TO OBEY	REWARDS FOR OBEDIENCE/ CONSEQUENCES OF DISOBEDIENCE/ SUPPORTING SCRIPTURES
1. *Do not use your freedom* to indulge in the sinful nature; *rather serve one another* in love. (see Gal.5:13/NIV)	For you, my brothers and sisters, are *called to be free.* (see Gal.5:13/NIV)
2. Love your neighbor as yourself. (see Gal.5:14/NIV)	For the entire law is summed up in a single command: "Love your neighbor as yourself." (see Gal.5:14/NIV)
3. Do not bite and devour each other. (see Gal.5:15/NIV)	Watch out *or you will be destroyed by each other.* (see Gal.5:15/NIV)

8.11 Be Led By The Holy Spirit & Not Be Under The Law

COMMANDMENTS OF GOD FOR US TO OBEY	REWARDS FOR OBEDIENCE/ CONSEQUENCES OF DISOBEDIENCE
1. Walk by the Spirit. (see Gal.5:16/NIV) 2. If we live by the Spirit, let us keep in step with the Spirit. (see Gal.5:25)	i. Then you will **not gratify the desires of the flesh.** (see Gal.5:16/NIV) ii. For the **flesh lusts against the Spirit,** and the Spirit against the flesh; and these are contrary to one another, so that you do not do the things that you wish. (see Gal.5:17) iii. If you live according to the flesh **you will die.** (see Rom.8:13) iv. But if by the Spirit, you put to death the deeds of the body, **you will live.** (see Rom.8:13)
3. **Be led by the Spirit.** (see Gal.5:18/NIV)	i. **Then you are not under the law.** (see Gal.5:18/NIV) ii. For as many as are led by the Spirit of God, these are **sons of God.** (see Rom.8:14) iii. **The "Fruit of the Spirit" is:** • Love, Joy, Peace • Patience, Kindness, Goodness • Faithfulness, Gentleness • Self-Control **Against such there is no law.** (see Gal.5:22-23)

8.12 The Lord Jesus Is The Spirit

(see 2 Cor.3:17)

Jesus Promises You Another Helper, The Holy Spirit
For Your Victorious Life on Earth *(see Rom.8:1-2)*

I. Who sends the Holy Spirit?

Jesus Himself sends the Holy Spirit, your Helper... Jesus stated, "I tell you the truth. It is to your advantage that I go away; for if I do not go away, *the Helper* will not come to you; but *if I depart, I will send Him to you.*" (see Jn.16:7)

II. Where does the Holy Spirit dwell?

*The Holy Spirit abides with you forever...*Jesus said, "The *Spirit of truth,* your helper, whom the world cannot receive, because it neither sees Him nor knows Him; but *you know Him,* for *He dwells with you and will be in you.*" (see Jn.14:16-17)

III. What does the Holy Spirit do for you?

- *The Holy Spirit helps you obey the Lord's Commandments...*Jesus said, "If you love Me, keep My commandments. And I will pray the Father, and He will give you *another Helper,* that He may abide with you forever." (see Jn.14:15-16)

- *The Holy Spirit teaches and reminds you of all of Jesus' Words...*Jesus declared, "The Helper, the Holy Spirit, whom the Father will send in My name, *He will teach you all things*, and bring to your remembrance all things that I said to you." (see Jn.14:25-26)

- *The Holy Spirit convicts the world of sin, of righteousness, and judgment...*Jesus explained, "The Spirit of truth will convict the world of sin, and of righteousness, and of judgment:

    i. of sin, because they do not believe in Me;

ii. of righteousness, because I go to My Father and you see Me no more;

iii. of judgment, because the ruler of this world, Satan, is judged." (see Jn.16:8-11)

iv. *Repent and be baptized* in the name of Jesus Christ for the forgiveness of your sins. And *you will receive the gift of the Holy Spirit.* (see Acts 2:38)

- *The Spirit of Truth guides you into all truth...*

    i. Jesus stated, "The Holy Spirit will not speak on His own authority,

    ii. but *whatever He hears He will speak*; and

    iii. He will tell you things to come.

    iv. *He will glorify Me,*

    v. for He will take of what is Mine and declare it to you."

    (see Jn.16:13-15)

- *The Holy Spirit gives you liberty...*Now the Lord is the Spirit; and where the Spirit of the Lord *is*, there *is* liberty. (see 2 Cor.3:17)

- *The Holy Spirit empowers you...* Jesus assured, "You shall *receive power* when the Holy Spirit comes upon you." (see Acts1:4-8)

- *The Holy Spirit helps you bear witness for Christ...*Jesus assured, "When the Helper comes, whom I shall send to you from the Father, the Spirit of truth who proceeds from the Father, He will testify of Me. And you also will bear witness. "(see Jn.15:26-27)

- *The Holy Spirit makes you witnesses of Jesus to all nations...* Jesus declared, "You shall be witnesses to Me in Jerusalem, and in all Judea and Samaria, and *to the end of the earth*." (see Acts 1:4-8)

IV. *When did Jesus breathe the Holy Spirit on His disciples?*

*Jesus equips His disciples for their Mission...*Jesus said to His disciples, "Peace to you! As the Father has sent Me, *I also send you.*"

And when He had said this, He breathed on them, and said to them, *"Receive the Holy Spirit.* (see Jn.20:21-22)

V. *How do you receive the Holy Spirit?*

Steps to follow... Ask, Wait, Tarry and Be Baptized with the Holy Spirit.

- *Ask...*Jesus declared "I say to you, ask, and it will be given to you; seek, and you will find; knock, and it will be opened to you.

- If a son asks for bread from any father among you, will he give him a stone? Or if *he asks* for a fish, will he give him a serpent instead of a fish? Or if he asks for an egg, will he offer him a scorpion?

  If *you then, being evil*, know how to give good gifts to your children, *how much more will your heavenly Father give the Holy Spirit to those who ask Him!"* (see Lk.11:9-13)

- *Wait for the promise, the Holy Spirit...*Jesus, being assembled together with the disciples, commanded them not to depart from Jerusalem, but to *wait for the Promise of the Father*, which," He said, "you have heard from Me." (see Acts 1:4-8)

- *Tarry until you are endued with the power of the Holy Spirit...*Jesus commanded His disciples, "Behold, I send the Promise of My Father upon you; but *tarry* in the city of Jerusalem until you are endued with power from on high." (see Lk.24:49)

- *Be baptized with the Holy Spirit...* Jesus declared, "For John truly baptized with water, but *you shall be baptized with the Holy Spirit* not many days from now." (see Acts 1:5)

VI. *Which fruit of the Holy Spirit will manifest through you?*

- *The Holy Spirit gives you the fruit of the Spirit...* The fruit of the Spirit is love, joy, peace, longsuffering, kindness, goodness, faithfulness, gentleness, self-control. (see Gal.5:22-23)

- *The Holy Spirit pours God's Love in your heart...*God's love is poured out into our hearts through the Holy Spirit, who has been given to us. (see Rom.5:5)

- *The Holy Spirit intercedes with divine love for the lost souls...* We do not know what we should pray for as we ought, but the *Spirit Himself makes intercession for us* and for the salvation of the lost souls with groanings which cannot be uttered. (see Rom.8:26)

- The Spirit of God makes intercession through you *for the saints according to the will of God.* (see Rom.8:27)

VII. *Why do you need the Holy Spirit in your life?*

- *The Holy Spirit delivers you from Condemnation of sin...* There is no condemnation to those who are in Christ Jesus, who *do not walk according to the flesh, but according to the Spirit.* (see Rom.8:1)

- *The Holy Spirit helps you lead a Victorious Life on earth...*For the law of the Spirit of life in Christ Jesus has made me *free from the law of sin and death.* The more of the Holy Spirit you have, the more you will be dead to sin. (see Rom.8:2)

- *The Holy Spirit makes you an over-comer...*The Holy Spirit helps you in your weaknesses to overcome the lust of the eyes, lust of the flesh and the pride of life. (see Rom. 8:26; 1 Jn.2:15-17)

- *The Holy Spirit guarantees your inheritance in Heaven...* In Christ, you are sealed with the Holy Spirit of promise, who is the *guarantee of your inheritance until the redemption* of the purchased possession (a believer). (see Eph.1:13-14; 2 Cor.5:5)

VIII. *To whom does the Lord give the Holy Spirit?*

- *"I will pour out My Spirit on all flesh...*before the coming of the great and awesome day of the LORD" declares the Lord God Almighty. You can claim this promise of the Lord for yourself and for your children since we are living in the last days. (see Joel 2:28, 31)

- *Believe in Christ and be sealed with the Holy Spirit of God...*When you hear the Word of Truth, the Gospel of your Salvation and believe in Christ, you are sealed with the Holy Spirit of promise. (see Eph.1:13)

IX. What increases the Anointing of the Holy Spirit on you?

- *Prayer brings down the Holy Spirit...*

  When you spend time in prayer, the Holy Spirit of God fills your spirit and you feel satisfied in your heart.

  In the Acts of the Apostles when the disciples prayed, *the place where they were assembled together was shaken*; and they were all *filled with the Holy Spirit,* and they spoke the word of God with boldness. (see Acts 1:12-2:4; 4:31)

- *Praying in the Spirit uplifts you...* When you pray in the Spirit, the anointing of the Holy Spirit increases upon you and edifies you. For the Scripture says that he who speaks in a tongue *edifies himself.* (see 1 Cor.14:4; Acts 2:1-4)

- *Thirst & Wait on the Lord to receive the rivers of Living Waters...*

  Jesus said, "If anyone *thirsts,* let him come to Me and drink. He who believes in Me, out of his heart will flow *rivers of Living Water.*" (Jn.7:37-38)

  The glory of God fills your heart when you wait on the Lord in the Most Holy Place early in the morning, preferably between 3am and 6am, when your mind is at rest.

- *God's Word Increases the Anointing...*

  Meditating the Word of God will increase the anointing on you and you will feel uplifted in your spirit. You will also experience the joy of the Holy Spirit in your heart.

  In the Acts of the Apostles, when the people *heard Peter preaching the Word of God,* they were cut to the heart and then Peter said to them, *"Repent,* and let every one of you be baptized in the name of Jesus Christ for the remission of sins; and you shall *receive the gift of the Holy Spirit.* (see Ps.19:7-11; Eph.1:13; Acts 2:14-38)

- *Obeying the call of God releases God's Power...*

  When you have a specific calling, as you yield, the Lord equips you with the power of the Holy Spirit to fulfill the call of God on your life.

For example, Peter was called to be a fisher of men. After receiving the power of the Holy Spirit at Pentecost, Peter preached the Word with boldness and three thousand people were saved in one day. (see Acts.2:41)

Similarly, from the Scriptures we know that people of God like **Moses, David, Samson, Prophet Ezekiel, Apostle Paul, Philip, Apostle John, Mary**, the Mother of Christ, etc., operated in the power of God and fulfilled their mission on earth.

- *Doing the will of God releases the Anointing...*

   Scripture says that God, our Savior, desires **all men to be saved** which is His perfect will. (see 1 Tim.2:4)

   When you please the Lord by standing in the gap and agonizing for lost souls, the Lord fills you with the rivers of Living Water and He increases the burden in your spirit to intercede for perishing souls.

- *Resisting Sin by yielding to the Holy Spirit increases the Anointing...*

   As long as you are willing to resist sin, the Lord will empower you with His Holy Spirit to overcome the temptation and not to be ensnared in that sin. (see 2 Cor.12:9)

- *Obedience to God's Commandments increases the Anointing...*

   When you obey the Commandments of God out of love for Christ, Jesus Christ Himself, along with Father God, will come and dwell in you. (see Jn.14:21, 23)

- *Suffering for Christ releases the Anointing...*

- When you suffer for Christ, His grace and anointing will be given to you to endure the sufferings for Him.

   The Lord said to Apostle Paul, *"**My grace** is sufficient for you, for **My power** is made perfect in weakness."* (see 2 Cor.12:9)

   The God of all grace, who called you to His eternal glory in Christ, after you have suffered a little while, will Himself restore you and make you strong, firm and steadfast. (1 Pet.5:10/NIV)

X. *How do you lose God's Anointing?*

You can leak out the anointing of the Holy Spirit...

- When you talk vain things and gossip about people.

- When you indulge in worldly pleasures, e.g., King David (see 2 Sam.11-12, Ps.51:1-12)

- When you willfully sin and rebel against God, e.g., King Saul (see 1 Sam. 13, 15)

- When you deliberately disobey God's Commandments, e.g., Samson (see Judges 14-16)

- *Depression & Sadness will overtake you...*Then you feel empty inside and depression and sadness fills your heart. That is the reason when King David committed the sin of adultery, he cried out to God to restore unto him the *joy of God's salvation* and to **uphold him with His generous Spirit**. (see Ps.51:10-12)

PART II

Commandments Of God From
The Book Of Ephesians

Book of Ephesians

Apostle Paul, a faithful servant of Jesus Christ, addressed this epistle to the Saints at Ephesus in Asia Minor. He wrote this letter in the year A.D. 62, most likely in Rome where he was a prisoner for his faith in Christ.

*The **Two Main Themes** of this Letter...*

- Redemption in Christ.
- New Life in Christ.

***Put it into practice**—*whatever you have learned, or received or heard from me, or seen in me," says Apostle Paul. (see Phil. 4:9/NIV)

1. Called To Live To The Praise of God's Glory

COMMANDMENTS OF GOD FOR US TO OBEY	REWARDS FOR OBEDIENCE/ SUPPORTING SCRIPTURES
1. *You, who trust in Christ, should live to the praise* of His Glory, as Apostle Paul stated. (see Eph.1:12)	*Why should we live to the praise of God's glory?* 1. For God has **blessed us** in the heavenly realms **with every spiritual blessing** in Christ. (see Eph.1:3/NIV) 2. For God **chose us** in Christ **before the creation** *of the world* **to be holy** and blameless in His sight. (see Eph.1:4/NIV) 3. In love, God **predestined us** to be **adopted as His sons** through Jesus Christ, in accordance **with His pleasure** and **will**. (see Eph.1:5/NIV) 4. God **predestined us** and adopted us as His sons **to the praise of His glorious grace.** (see Eph.1:6/NIV) 5. God has *freely given us His glorious grace* in the One He loves, Jesus Christ. (see Eph.1:6/NIV) 6. In Christ, we have **redemption through His blood**. (see Eph.1:7/NIV) 7. In Christ, we have the *forgiveness of sins,* in accordance with the *riches of God's grace* that He *lavished on us* with all wisdom and understanding (knowing our rebellious nature). (see Eph.1:8/NIV)

COMMANDMENTS OF GOD	REWARDS FOR OBEDIENCE/ SUPPORTING SCRIPTURES
1. *You, who trust in Christ, should live to the praise* of His Glory, as Apostle Paul stated. (see Eph.1:12)	8. God *made known to us the mystery of His will* according to His *good pleasure* which He purposed in Christ. (see Eph.1:9/NIV)
	9. God made known to us the *mystery of His will* to be put into effect when the times reach their fulfillment—*to bring all things* in heaven and on earth together *under one head, even Christ Jesus.* (see Eph.1:10/NIV)
	10. In Christ, we *of God* who works all things according to the counsel of His will. (see Eph.1:11)
	Praise be to the God and Father of our Lord Jesus Christ who has blessed us with all the above spiritual blessings in Christ. (see Eph.1:3/NIV)
2. Hear the Word of Truth, the gospel of your salvation, as Apostle Paul stated. (see Eph.1:13)	Then you will trust in Christ.— Apostle Paul. (see Eph.1:13)

1.1 How Can We Live To The Praise Of God's Glory?

Holy Spirit, the Guarantee of Your Inheritance In Heaven…We can live to the praise of God's glory only by the power of the Holy Spirit.

COMMANDMENTS OF GOD FOR US TO OBEY	REWARDS FOR OBEDIENCE/ SUPPORTING SCRIPTURES
1. Believe in Christ, as Apostle Paul says. (see Eph.1:12-13/NIV)	i. *When you believe in Christ…*You are *sealed with the Holy Spirit* of promise, who is the *guarantee* of your inheritance until the redemption of the purchased possession, *to the praise of His glory.* (see Eph.1:14)
	ii. The Spirit also *helps in our weaknesses.* (see Rom.8:26)
	iii For we do not know what we should pray for as we ought, but the *Spirit Himself makes intercession for us* with groaning which cannot be uttered. (see Rom.8:26)
	iv. Now He who searches the hearts knows what the mind of the Spirit *is,* because He *makes intercession for the saints according to the will of God.* (see Rom.8:26-27)
2. *You are created in Christ for good works…* Do good works, which God prepared in advance for us to do. (see Eph.2:10/NIV)	i. For you are God's workmanship, created in Christ Jesus to do good works. (see Eph.2:10)
	ii. Let your light so shine before men, that *they may see your good works, and glorify your Father* who is in heaven. (see Matt.5:16/KJV)

Pause & Think!

- The Holy Spirit not only guarantees your inheritance in heaven but also helps you to overcome *your weaknesses on earth* thereby enabling you to live to the praise of His glory. (see Eph.1:14; Rom.8:26-27)

- After you believe in Christ and accept Him as your Lord and Savior, only then the good works which you do on earth will be credited to your account for your rewards in Heaven.

- *Every good work that you do after your Salvation counts* and is written in the books in Heaven (Books of Good and Evil) and you will be rewarded accordingly on the day of Judgment. (see Eccl. 12:14; 2 Cor.5:10; Rev.20:12)

1.2 The Exceeding Greatness Of God's Power Available To Believers In Christ

I. The incomparable great power of the Holy Spirit that is available to us, believers, is like the working of **God's mighty power, which He exerted in Christ...**

i. when God raised Christ from the dead;

ii. when God seated Christ at His right hand in the heavenly realms,

iii. *far above all rule, and authority, and power, and dominion, and*

iv. *far above every name that is named,*

v. not only in this world, but also in that which is to come; and

vi. **God has put all things under Christ's feet; and**

vii. God appointed **Christ to be Head** over everything for the church, which is His body.

viii. The *fullness of Christ fills all in all.* (see Eph.1:19-23)

II. **You Too Can Receive His Awesome Power...**Can you imagine that this awesome power of the Holy Spirit that worked in Christ Jesus is also available to us, the faithful believers?

Jesus exhorts us to **keep on asking, seeking and knocking** at Heaven's door *until you receive the fullness of the Holy Spirit;* for Jesus Himself prayed fervently and received the **Holy Spirit without measure.** (see Matt. 7:7; Jn. 3:34; Luke 3:21-22; 11:9-13)

As a believer, if you are still in bondage and have not overcome sin, Satan and the world, as Jesus did, it means that *you are not using the fullness of the power of the Holy Spirit* that is available to you. How sad!

2. How Not To Live In The Futility Of The Mind

*Spirit, Soul & Body...*We, human beings, are made up of spirit, soul (mind) and body. Scientists say that our spirit which is lodged in between our rib cage weighs about 21 grams. (1 Thes.5:23)

*Spirit saved at Salvation...*When we accept Christ as our Savior, only our spirit is saved and it is saved forever, unless otherwise we rebel against God and choose to lose our Salvation, like Judas did.

*Soul being saved life long...*Our soul, which deals with our feelings, emotions, thought life, intelligence and will power, is being saved throughout our life. (see James 1:21; 1Pet.1:8-9)

Body saved at Resurrection... Once our spirit is saved, we should guard our Salvation with fear and trembling all our life, then our body will be saved in the resurrection, when we put on immortality. (see Phil.2:12; 1 Cor.15:42-55)

*Watch out! Satan influences our Mind through our five senses...*If we are not careful and if we allow our mind to be corrupted with the filth of this world, then heed the warning of the Lord. He **warns us by saying, Why should you be beaten anymore? Your whole head is sick,** and your whole heart is afflicted. From the top of your head to the soles of your feet, there is no soundness, but wounds and bruises and putrefying sores; they have not been closed or bound up, or **soothed with healing ointment of God's Word.** (see Is.1:5-6; Prov.3:8)

*Repent or else the Lord will not hear your Prayers...*If we don't repent, change our ways and fill our minds with the pure, holy and righteous thoughts, then the Lord says to us, "When you spread out your hands, I will hide My eyes from you; even though **you make many prayers, I will not hear.**" (see Is. 1:15; Phil.4:8)

Heed the Warning of the Lord today..."Wash yourselves, make yourselves clean. **If you are willing and obedient, you shall eat the good of the land;** but if you refuse and *rebel, you shall be devoured by the sword"*; for the mouth of the Lord has spoken this. (see Is. 1:16, 19-20)

*Either be hot or cold but not lukewarm...*If we continue to fill our mind with vain, unrighteous, impure, immoral or lustful thoughts, eventually *we will leak out the Anointing of the Holy Spirit* and we will become neither hot nor cold but lukewarm and the Lord says that *He will spit us out of His mouth.* So let us heed the warning of the Lord today. (see Rev.3:15-16)

Commandments concerning the following topics given in this Chapter will help you not to live in the futility of your Mind:

- Put off your former way of life
- When you defile your mind you offer defiled sacrifice to the Lord
- Be renewed in the spirit of your mind
- How to put on the new self
- Consequences of drinking Wine

2.1 Put Off Your Former Way Of Life

COMMANDMENTS OF GOD	CONSEQUENCES OF DISOBEDIENCE
1. You, no longer live *as the Gentiles do*, in the futility of their *thinking.* (see Eph.4:17/NIV)	i. For the Gentiles (unbelievers) are *darkened* in their *understanding.* (see Eph.4:18/NIV)
2. You, put off your former way of life, your old self, which is being corrupted by its deceitful desires. (see Eph.4:22/NIV)	ii. *They are separated from the Life of God* because of the *ignorance* that is in them due to the *hardening of their hearts.* (see Eph.4:18/NIV)
	iii. Having *lost all sensitivity*, they have given themselves over to *sensuality,* so as to indulge in every kind of *impurity*, with the *continual lust* for more. (see Eph.4:19/NIV)
	iv. However, this is not the way of life you (believers) learned when you heard about Christ and were taught in Him in accordance with the truth that is in Jesus. (see Eph.4:20-21/NIV)
3. *Do not follow the ways of this world,* and of the ruler of the kingdom of the air, *the evil spirit* who is now at work in those who are *disobedient*. (see Eph.2:2/NIV)	Or else, you will *die in your transgressions* and sins. (see Eph.2:1-2/NIV)

2.2 When You Defile Your Mind You Offer Defiled Sacrifice To The Lord

- *"Do Not Offer Defiled Sacrifice On My Altar,"* says the Lord of Hosts. (see Mal.1:7-8)

- Brethren, you **present your bodies a living sacrifice**, holy, acceptable unto God. (see Rom.12:1)

- *Walk worthy of your calling...*

  When you want to please God at any cost and desire to fulfill His will for your life, then you should be very careful with your walk with the Lord.

- *Do not rebel against God...*If you don't guard your heart and harbor even a little disappointment against the Lord, you will tend to rebel against Him. Immediately, Satan, the deceiver, will try to **distract you with the things of the world.** (see 2 Cor.11:3).

- *How do you defile your mind?*

- *Satan attacks your mind...*If the devil cannot make you fall into big temptations, he will divert you by attacking your mind in a subtle way. You should be careful what you fill your mind with; *for as a man thinks, so shall he be.* (see Prov.23:7)

  Do not corrupt your mind by watching filthy, lustful, perverse or sexually immoral scenes from movies, TV, internet, cell phones, etc., which **affect your sensuality and emotions.** This is sinful in the eyes of God. Even though it may seem to be a light entertainment to you, it defiles your mind. And the **carnal mind is enmity against God.** (see Rom.8:7)

- *You are the temple of the Holy Spirit...*

  Since Christ is enthroned in your heart, do you think the Lord can watch those sensual scenes with you? The Lord says, "Do Not Offer Defiled Sacrifice On My Altar"; Is it not evil? *Offer it to your governor!* Would he be pleased with you? (see Mal.1:7-9)

- *You may lose God's Favor...*

When you offer defiled sacrifice i.e. your corrupted mind to the Lord, and then you entreat God's favor, He may not be gracious to you. He will not accept you favorably. (see Mal.1:7-9)

- *Consequences, if you do not renew your mind...*

If you ignore the repeated convictions of the Holy Spirit and persist in the futility of your thinking, then you will face the following consequences...

1. You will be *darkened* in your *understanding*.

2. You will be *separated from the Life of God*. and become dead in your spirit by leaking out the Holy Spirit from within you.

3. You will be *ignorant of God's ways and lose God's blessings*.

4. Your *heart will become hardened*.

5. You will *lose all sensitivity to the Holy Spirit*.

6. You will give yourself over to *sensuality,* so as to indulge in every kind of *impurity*, with the *continual lust* for more. (see Eph.4:18-19/NIV; 1 Cor.7:5)

- *Sanctify your mind...*

*The Word of God renews your mind...*Therefore, be transformed by renewing your mind constantly with the pure Word of God. (see Rom.12:2; Jn. 17:17)

The Holy Spirit governs your mind... The mind governed by the Spirit is life and peace but the mind governed by the flesh is death. (see Rom.8:6/NIV)

2.3 Be Renewed In The Spirit Of Your Mind

COMMANDMENTS OF GOD FOR US TO OBEY	REWARDS FOR OBEDIENCE/ SUPPORTING SCRIPTURES
1. Be renewed in the spirit of your mind. (see Eph. 4:23) 2. You, **put on the new self,** created to be like God, in true righteousness and holiness. —Apostle Paul. (see Eph. 4:24/NIV) 3. Do not conform any longer to the pattern of this world; but be transformed by the *renewing of your mind (with the Word of God).* —Apostle Paul. (see Rom.12:2; Phil.4:8/NIV)	For you, believers, were taught in accordance with **the truth that is in Jesus.** So be made new in the **attitude** of your minds. —Apostle Paul. (see Eph. 4:21-23/NIV)

Some of the ways you can renew your mind…

- **Think on true and pure things…**

  Finally, brethren,

  whatsoever things are *true,*

  whatsoever things are *honest,*

  whatsoever things are *just,*

  whatsoever things are *pure,*

  whatsoever things are *lovely,*

  whatsoever things are of *good report;*

  if there be any virtue, and if there be any praise, *think on these things.* (Phil.4:8/KJV)

- *Meditate on God's Word day and night…*Scripture also says, delight in the law of the Lord and meditate on His Word day and night. For God's Word is true, honest, just, pure, lovely and of good report. (see Ps.1:2; 119)

- ***Bring every wrong thought captive to the obedience of Christ…***We demolish arguments and every pretension that sets itself up against the knowledge of God, and we take captive every thought to make it obedient to Christ. (2 Cor.10:5/NIV)

2.4 How To Put On The New Self

(Fruits of New Self)

If anyone is in Christ, he is a new creation; old things have passed away; behold, all things have become new. (2 Cor. 5:17)

When you obey the following commandments, the fruits of the new self will manifest in your life.

COMMANDMENTS OF GOD FOR US TO OBEY	REWARDS FOR OBEDIENCE/ CONSEQUENCES OF DISOBEDIENCE
Truthfulness: 1. Put away lying, and let each one of you speak truth with his neighbor. (see Eph. 4:25)	For we are all members of one Body. (see Eph. 4:25/NIV)
Put Away Anger: 2. (i) In your anger, do not sin. (ii) Do not let the sun go down while you are still angry. (see Eph. 4:26/NIV)	Or else you will give **place to the devil**. (see Eph. 4:27)
Steal No Longer: 3. Let him who stole steal no longer, but rather let him labor, working with his hands what is good. (see Eph. 4:28)	So that he may have something to share with those in need. (see Eph.4:28/NIV)
No Corrupt Communication: 4. Do not let any unwholesome talk come out of your mouths, but only what is helpful for building others up according to their needs. (see Eph.4:29/NIV)	So that it may benefit those who listen. (see Eph.4:29/NIV)
Grieve Not the Holy Spirit: 5. Do not grieve the Holy Spirit of God. (see Eph.4:30)	By whom you were sealed for the day of redemption. (see Eph.4:30)

COMMANDMENTS OF GOD FOR US TO OBEY	REWARDS FOR OBEDIENCE/ CONSEQUENCES OF DISOBEDIENCE
No Bitterness, Hatred, etc. 6. Get rid of all bitterness, rage and anger, brawling and slander, along with every form of malice. (see Eph.4:31/NIV)	A gentle answer turns away wrath, but a harsh word stirs up anger. (see Prov.15:1/NIV)
Kindness & Forgiveness: 7. Be kind and compassionate to one another, forgiving each other. (see Eph.4:32/NIV)	Just as in Christ God forgave you. (see Eph.4:32/NIV)
Life of Love: 8. Be imitators of God, as dearly loved children and live a life of love. (see Eph.5:1-2/NIV)	Just as Christ loved us and gave Himself up for us as a fragrant offering and sacrifice to God. (see Eph.5:2/NIV)
No Sexual Immorality & Greed: 9. Fornication and all uncleanness or covetousness, let it not even be named among you. (see Eph.5:3)	Because these are improper for God's holy people. (see Eph.5:3/NIV)
No Obscenity & Foolish Talk: 10. Let there not be obscenity, foolish talk or coarse joking, which are out of place but rather thanksgiving. (see Eph.5:4/NIV)	For no immoral, impure or greedy person—such a man is an idolater—has any **inheritance in the Kingdom of Christ** and of God. (see Eph.5:5/NIV)
No Deception: 11(i) Let no one deceive you with empty words. (see Eph.5:6/NIV) (ii) Do not be partners with them. (see Eph.5:7/NIV)	For because of such things **God's wrath** comes on those who are **disobedient**. (see Eph.5:6/NIV)

*Point to Ponder…*Paul explains here that certain people might deceive you into believing that one can have an unrighteous lifestyle and still make it to Heaven which is not true. He warns us not to be partners with such people.

COMMANDMENTS OF GOD FOR US TO OBEY	REWARDS FOR OBEDIENCE/ CONSEQUENCES OF DISOBEDIENCE
Be Children of Light: 12 (i) Live as children of light. (see Eph.5:8/NIV) (ii) And **find out what pleases the Lord**. (see Eph.5:10/NIV)	i. For you were once darkness, but now you are light in the Lord. (Eph.5:8/NIV) ii. For the fruit of the light consists in all goodness, righteousness and truth. (see Eph.5:9/NIV)
Get rid of Fruitless Deeds: 13. Have nothing to do with the fruitless deeds of darkness, but rather expose them. (see Eph.5:11/NIV)	i. For *it is shameful even to mention what the disobedient do in secret.* (see Eph.5:12/NIV) ii. Everything exposed by the light becomes visible. iii. For it is *light that makes everything visible.* (see Eph.5:13/NIV)
Rise from the dead: 14. *Wake up, O sleeper;* rise from the dead. (see Eph.5:14/NIV)	And Christ will shine on you. (see Eph.5:14/NIV)
Redeem your time: 15 (i) Be very careful, how you live—not as unwise but as wise making the most of every opportunity. (see Eph.5:15-16/NIV) (ii) Redeem your time. (Eph.5:16)	*Because the days are evil.* (see Eph.5:15-16)

COMMANDMENTS OF GOD FOR US TO OBEY	REWARDS FOR OBEDIENCE/ CONSEQUENCES OF DISOBEDIENCE
Discern God's Will: 16. Do not be foolish but understand what the Lord's will is. (see Eph.5:17/NIV)	*Ask God to fill you with the knowledge of His will* through all spiritual wisdom and understanding; in order that you may live a life worthy of the Lord and may please Him in every way. (see Col.1:9-10/NIV)
Avoid Alcoholism: 17 (i) *Do not get drunk on wine.* (see Eph.5:18/NIV)	Which leads to *debauchery i.e., wickedness.* (see Eph.5:18/NIV)
(ii) *Do not look at wine* when it is red, when it sparkles in the cup and goes down smoothly. (see Prov.23:29-35)	i. In the end *it bites like a serpent* and stings like an adder. ii. Your eyes will *see strange things.* iii. And your heart *utter perverse things.* (see Prov.23:29-35)

2.5 Consequences of Drinking Wine

1. *Wine* is a *mocker,* strong drink a *brawler,* and whoever is led astray by it is *not wise.* (see Prov.20:1)

2. *Woe to those* who are heroes at *drinking wine,* and valiant men in mixing *strong drink.* (see Is.5:22)

3. *Who has woe?*

    Who has *sorrow?*

    Who has *strife?*

    Who has complaining?

    Who has *wounds* without cause?

    Who has redness of eyes?

    Those who tarry long over wine; those who go to try mixed wine. (see Prov.23:29-35)

4. Woe to those *who rise early in the morning that they may* run after strong drink, *who tarry late into the evening as wine inflames them! (see Is.5:11)*

5. *Eternal Damnation for Drunkenness...*

    The works of the flesh are evident, which are: adultery, fornication, uncleanness, lewdness, idolatry, sorcery, hatred, contentions, jealousies, outbursts of wrath, selfish ambitions, dissensions, heresies, envy, murders, *drunkenness,* revelries, and the like; and those who practice such things *will not inherit the kingdom of God.* (see Gal.5:19-21)

6. *The Holy Spirit Will Deliver You From Alcoholism...*

    The Scripture says, do not get drunk on wine; *instead, be filled with the Holy Spirit of God*; for He is the real joy giver. (see Eph.5:18/NIV; Rom.14:17; Jn. 16:24)

    The Holy Spirit is the one who can help you overcome the addiction of alcoholism; *for the Spirit helps in your weaknesses.* (see Rom.8:26)

2.6 Fruits of New Self—Be Filled With The Holy Spirit

COMMANDMENTS OF GOD FOR US TO OBEY	REWARDS FOR OBEDIENCE/ SUPPORTING SCRIPTURES
Infilling of the Holy Spirit: 18 (i) Be filled with the Spirit. (see Eph.5:18/NIV) (ii) Be baptized with the Holy Spirit. (see Acts 1:4-5)	i. The disciples were *all filled with the Holy Spirit and began to speak in other tongues* as the Spirit gave them utterance. (see Acts. 2:1-47) ii. You will *receive power* when the Holy Spirit comes upon you and you will *be My witnesses*.—Jesus. (see Acts 1:8)

2.7 Fruits of New Self–Sing Unto The Lord

COMMANDMENTS OF GOD FOR US TO OBEY	REWARDS FOR OBEDIENCE/ SUPPORTING SCRIPTURES
Spiritual Songs: 19. Speak to one another with psalms, hymns and spiritual songs. (see Eph.5:19)	*Let the Word of Christ dwell in you* richly as you teach and admonish one another with all wisdom, and *as you sing psalms, hymns* and *spiritual songs* with gratitude in your hearts to God. (see Col.3:16/NIV)
Sing unto the Lord: 20. (i) Sing and make music from your heart to the Lord. (ii) Always give thanks to God the Father for everything in the Name of our Lord Jesus Christ. (see Eph.5:19-20/NIV)	"I will sing with my spirit, and I will also sing with my understanding," says apostle Paul. (see 1 Cor.14:15/NIV)
Reverence for Christ: 21. Submit to one another out of reverence for Christ. (see Eph.5:21/NIV)	Be kindly affectionate to one another with **brotherly love,** in honor giving **preference** to one another. (see Rom.12:10)

3. Jews & Gentiles Both Reconciled To God By The Cross Of Christ

*Gentiles Brought Near To God By The Blood of Christ...*Apostle Paul says, "Remember that formerly you who are Gentiles by birth and called "**uncircumcised**" by those (Jews) who call themselves "the circumcision" which is done in the body by human hands;

Remember that at that time *you, gentiles, were separated from Christ*, excluded from citizenship in Israel and foreigners to the covenants of the promise, without hope and *without God in the world*. (Eph.2:11-13/NIV)

*Mystery of Christ revealed...*Now the mystery of Christ has been revealed that the Jews and Gentiles are one in Jesus Christ and the gentiles should be fellow heirs, of the same body, and partakers of God's promise in Christ through the Gospel. (see Eph.3:3-6)

COMMANDMENTS OF GOD FOR US TO OBEY	REWARDS FOR OBEDIENCE/ SUPPORTING SCRIPTURES
To The Gentile Believers:	*As Gentile Believers, in Christ Jesus,*
Do not be strangers and foreigners any longer, but *fellow citizens with the saints* and members of the household of God.—Apostle Paul. (see Eph.2:19)	1. You are no longer strangers from the *covenants of promise*. (see Eph. 2:12) 2. You are now *with hope* and *with God* in the world. (see Eph. 2:12) 3. You who once were far off, *are brought near by the blood of Christ*. (see Eph. 2:13) 4. For *Christ Himself is our peace*, who has made both (Jews and Gentiles) one and has *broken down the middle wall of separation*. (see Eph.2:14)

COMMANDMENTS OF GOD FOR US TO OBEY	CONSEQUENCES OF DISOBEDIENCE/ SUPPORTING SCRIPTURES
To The Gentile Believers: Do not be strangers and foreigners any longer, but *fellow citizens with the saints* and members of the household of God.—Apostle Paul. (see Eph.2:19)	5. For Christ has *abolished in His flesh the enmity*, so as to create in Himself **one new man** *from the two* (Jews and Gentiles), *thus making peace.* (see Eph.2:15) 6. For Christ has *reconciled them both to God* in one body through the cross, thereby putting to death the enmity. (see Eph.2:16) 7. For through Christ, we *both (Jews & Gentiles) have access by one Spirit to the Father.* (see Eph.2:18) 8. Now you, gentiles, are being *built on the foundation of the apostles and prophets*, Jesus Christ Himself being the chief cornerstone. (see Eph.2:20) 9. For in Christ, the chief cornerstone, the whole building, being fitted together, grows into a holy temple in the Lord, in whom you, (gentiles) also are being built together for *a dwelling place of God in the Spirit.*—Apostle Paul. (see Eph.2:21-22) 10. *The mystery of Christ* is that the *gentiles* should be *fellow heirs* of the same body and *partakers of God's promise* in Christ through the gospel. (see Eph.3:4-6)

Every believer in Christ on earth, other than the
Jews, is called a gentile believer.

3.1 Preach The Unsearchable Riches Of Christ

Christ ascended far above all the heavens, that *He might fill all things*. And in Christ, *we live and move and have our being*. (see Eph.4:10; Acts 17:28)

COMMANDMENTS OF GOD FOR US TO OBEY	REWARDS FOR OBEDIENCE/ SUPPORTING SCRIPTURES
1. Preach the *unsearchable riches of Christ*. (see Eph.3:8)	i. For God *created all things through Jesus Christ*. (see Eph.3:9)
2. Make all see the *fellowship of the mystery of Christ*, as Apostle Paul did. (see Eph.3:8)	ii. God's intent is that now the *manifold wisdom of God* might be *made known by the church* to the principalities and *powers in the heavenly places*; according to the *eternal purpose* which God accomplished in Christ Jesus our Lord. (see Eph.3:10-11)
	iii. For we have *boldness and access to God with confidence* through faith in Christ.—Apostle Paul. (see Eph.3:12)

The mystery of Christ is that God purposed in His heart to bring all people, both Jews and Gentiles into salvation through faith in Jesus Christ. (see Eph.3:6)

3.2 Eternal Purpose of God Through Christ Revealed To The Heavenly Hosts By The Church

*The principalities and powers in heavenly places...*This may refer to good angels or demonic spirits.

The angels in heaven now understand that God's eternal purpose in sending His only begotten Son, Jesus Christ to earth was *to redeem all of mankind through His sacrifice on the cross*. All of heaven marvels at this manifold wisdom of God as He demonstrates that wisdom through the church. (see Col.1:16)

The principalities and powers in heavenly places may also refer to the ruling powers of darkness in the spiritual realm to whom God's eternal purpose is being made known that God has accomplished the *redemption plan through the cross of Christ* to save all of mankind, *as the churches proclaim this salvation message of Jesus Christ* all over the world. (see Eph.6:12-18; 2 Cor.10:4-5)

4. Pray As Apostle Paul Prayed

The prayer of Apostle Paul indicates *God's highest desire* for every believer in Christ.

Paul did not pray for the personal needs of believers; rather he prayed that they should walk in the fullness of the Spirit. From his prayers, we learn that we also should *pray more for the things of the above* than for the earthly things, like house, car, career, etc.

Apostle Paul says...

"Join together in following my example, brothers and sisters, and just as you have *us as a model*, keep your eyes on those who live as we do." (see Phil.3:17)

Be ye followers of me, even as I also am of Christ. (see 1 Cor.11:1/KJV)

Put it into practice—whatever you have *learned, or received or heard* from me, or *seen in me*." (see Phil 4:9/NIV)

Therefore let us follow Apostle Paul's example and pray as he prayed.

4.1 Pray For The Spirit Of Wisdom & Revelation In the Knowledge of God

COMMANDMENTS OF GOD FOR US TO OBEY	REWARDS FOR OBEDIENCE
Pray that the God of our Lord Jesus Christ, the Father of glory, may give to you— i. the Spirit of wisdom and ii. Revelation in the knowledge of Him, as apostle Paul prayed. (see Eph.1:16-17)	So that you may *know Him better.* (see Eph.1:17/NIV)

4.2 Pray That Your Spiritual Eyes Be Opened

"Blessed are your eyes for they see," said the Lord Jesus to His disciples. (see Matt.13:16)

COMMANDMENTS OF GOD FOR US TO OBEY	REWARDS FOR OBEDIENCE
Pray that the eyes of your heart be enlightened, as apostle Paul prayed. (see Eph.1:18/NIV)	In order that you may know... i. what is the *hope of His calling,* ii. what are the *riches of His glorious inheritance* in the saints and iii. what is the *exceeding greatness of His power toward us* who believe. (see Eph.1:18-19)

4.3 Pray To Be Strengthened By The Holy Spirit

COMMANDMENTS OF GOD FOR US TO OBEY	REWARDS FOR OBEDIENCE
Pray that out of His glorious riches, God may **strengthen you with power through His Spirit in your inner being,** as apostle Paul prayed. (see Eph.3:16/NIV)	So that **Christ may dwell in your hearts** through faith.—Apostle Paul. (see Eph.3:17/NIV)

4.4 Pray To Comprehend Christ's Love For You

COMMANDMENTS OF GOD FOR US TO OBEY	REWARDS FOR OBEDIENCE/ SUPPORTING SCRIPTURES
1. *Pray that, being rooted and established in love...* i. you may have **power,** together with all the saints, *to grasp how wide and long and high and deep is the love of Christ*, and ii. you may **know** this love that surpasses knowledge, as apostle Paul prayed. (see Eph.3:17-19/NIV)	i. So that you may be *filled with all the fullness of God.* (see Eph.3:19) ii. For God is *able to do exceedingly abundantly above all* that we *ask or think,* according to the *power* that works in us. (see Eph.3:20) iii. Now *to God be glory in the church* and in Christ Jesus to all generations *forever and ever.* (see Eph.3:21)
Let your love for Christ abound more and more... 2. Pray that your love may abound more and more in knowledge and *depth of insight,* as Apostle Paul prayed. (see Phil. 1:9/NIV)	*So that...* i. you may be able to *discern what is best;* ii. you may be *pure and blameless* until the day of Christ; and iii. you may be filled with the *fruit of righteousness* that comes through Jesus Christ—to the glory and praise of God. (see Phil. 1:10-11/NIV)

4.5 Grace To All Who Love Our Lord Jesus Christ With An Undying Love!

- *Everlasting Love of God...* The Lord says, "I have loved you with an everlasting love; therefore **with loving kindness I have drawn you.**" (see Jer.31:3)

- *The unconditional love of Jesus...Jesus loves you so much* that He died in your place and took the penalty of your sins upon Himself. He loves you just as you are.

- *"Remain in My Love"...* Jesus says, *"As the Father has loved Me*, so have *I loved you.* Now remain in My love." (see Jn.15:9/NIV)

- *Your deep love for Christ...* First you should comprehend how wide and long and high and deep is Christ's love for you, then you must pray that your love for Christ may abound more and more.

- *Your passion for Christ will make you live a holy life....* When you have an undying love for your Bridegroom, Jesus Christ, then you will desire to live a righteous, pure and blameless life until you meet Him face to face; for you will never want to grieve His loving heart.

- *"If you love Me, keep My Commandments,"* says Jesus. If you truly love the Lord Jesus, then it will be easy for you to obey His Commandments. (Jn.14:15)

4.6 Pray To Be Filled With The Knowledge Of God's Will

Jesus warns: "Not everyone who says to Me, 'Lord, Lord,' shall **enter the Kingdom of Heaven, but he who does the will of My Father** in heaven. Many will say to Me in that day, 'Lord, Lord, have we not prophesied in Your name, cast out demons in Your name, and done many wonders in Your name?' And then I will declare to them, '**I never knew you; depart from Me, you who practice lawlessness!**' (see Matt.7:21-23)

COMMANDMENTS OF GOD FOR US TO OBEY	REWARDS FOR OBEDIENCE/ SUPPORTING SCRIPTURES
1. Pray that you may be filled with the knowledge of God's will in all wisdom and spiritual understanding, as Apostle Paul prayed. (see Col.1:9)	So that... i. You may live a **life worthy of the Lord,** (see Col. 1:10/NIV) ii. You may **please Him in every way.** (see Col. 1:10/NIV) iii. You may **bear fruit** in every good work. (see Col. 1:10/NIV) iv. You may **grow in the knowledge of God.** (see Col. 1:10/NIV) v. You may **be strengthened with all power** according to His glorious might, so that you may **have great endurance and patience.**—Apostle Paul (see Col. 1:11/NIV)
2. You, **joyfully give thanks** to the Father, as Apostle Paul did. (see Col. 1:12/NIV)	i. For God has qualified you to share in the **inheritance of the saints** in the Kingdom of light. (see Col. 1:12/NIV) ii. For God has **rescued you from the dominion of darkness** and brought you into the Kingdom of the Son He loves.—Apostle Paul. (see Col. 1:13/NIV) iii. In Christ, you have **redemption,** the forgiveness of sins. (see Col. 1:14/NIV)

4.7 Pray That You May Be Encouraged In Heart

COMMANDMENTS OF GOD FOR US TO OBEY	REWARDS FOR OBEDIENCE/
Pray that you may be encouraged in heart and united in love. -Apostle Paul (see Col.2:2/NIV)	1. So that you may have the *full riches* of *complete understanding.* (see Col.2:2/NIV)
	2. In order that you may *know the mystery of God, namely, Christ*, in whom are *hidden all the treasures* of wisdom and knowledge. (see Col.2:2-3/NIV)
	3. So that *no one may deceive you* by fine-sounding arguments.— Apostle Paul (see Col.2:4/NIV)

Points to Ponder...

- **Be Encouraged in Heart:** Strengthen your inner man...

    i.   by having **intimate relationship with Christ** through prayer

    ii. by meditating on the **Word of God**

    iii. by **obeying the Commandments of God** and

    iv. by the **infilling of the Holy Spirit**

    v.   so that you will **understand the fullness of Jesus Christ**, the mystery of God, in whom all the treasures of wisdom and knowledge are hidden.

- **Be united in love...**Apostle Paul is exhorting the believers to be united in love and to edify one another in faith so that we can grow together in the complete understanding of who Christ is and how good and loving God is.

- Then you will not be deceived by the enticing words of men.

5. Submit To One Another In The Fear Of God

Commandments regarding the following topics will enable you to have a Godly, healthy family unit:

- Children, Honor Your Father & Mother To Enjoy Long Life
- Husband & Wife - One Flesh, A Profound Mystery
- God Instituted Marriage Between A Man & A Woman
- Servants & Masters - Remember, Your Master is in Heaven!

*Godly family...*God has established the family as the basic unit in society. Mutual submission in Christ is an important spiritual principle that every Christian family should follow.

In order to live the abundant life intended by the Lord God Almighty, each member of the family must exhibit the characteristics of *submission, humility, gentleness, patience and respect for each other.*

5.1 Children, Honor Your Father & Mother To Enjoy Long Life

COMMANDMENTS OF GOD FOR US TO OBEY	REWARDS FOR OBEDIENCE/ SUPPORTING SCRIPTURES
1. Children, *Obey* your parents in the Lord. (see Eph.6:1/NIV)	For this is right. (see Eph.6:1)
2. Honor your father and mother. (see Eph.6:2/NIV)	For this is the first commandment with the promise that - i. it may *go well with you* and ii. you may *enjoy long life* on the earth. (see Eph.6:2-3/NIV)
To The Fathers... *3. Fathers,* do not provoke your children to wrath.(see Eph.6:4)	Instead, bring them up in the training and instruction of the Lord. (see Eph.6:4/NIV)

Children should honor and obey their father and mother since *parents are the pride of their children.* (see Prov.17:6)

5.2 Husband & Wife—One Flesh, A Profound Mystery

COMMANDMENTS OF GOD FOR US TO OBEY	REWARDS FOR OBEDIENCE/ SUPPORTING SCRIPTURES
Wives... 1. Wives, submit to your own husbands, as to the Lord. (see Eph.5:22) 2. Wives, respect your husbands. (see Eph.5:33/NIV)	i. For the husband is the head of the wife, *as Christ is the head of the church,* His body, of which He is the Savior. (see Eph.5:23/NIV) ii. Now *as the church submits to Christ,* so also wives should submit to their husbands in everything. (see Eph.5:24/NIV)

A man will leave his father and mother and be united to his wife. And the *two will become one flesh.* This is a *profound mystery* about *Christ and the church.* (see Eph.5:31-32/NIV)

COMMANDMENTS OF GOD FOR US TO OBEY	REWARDS FOR OBEDIENCE/ SUPPORTING SCRIPTURES
Husbands... 1. Husbands, love your wives, just as Christ loved the church. (see Eph.5:25/NIV)	*How to love your wife?* *1. As Christ loved the Church...* i. For *Christ gave Himself up for the church* to make her holy, ii. cleansing the church by the washing with water through the Word, iii. and *to present her to Himself* as a radiant church, without stain or wrinkle or any other blemish, but *holy and blameless.* (see Eph.5:25-27/NIV) 2. In this same way, husbands ought to love their wives *as their own bodies*. (see Eph.5:28/NIV) 3. Each one of you must love his wife *as he loves himself.* (see Eph.5:33/NIV)
2. Husbands, love your wives as your own bodies. (see Eph.5:28/NIV) 3. Each one of you *must love* his wife as he loves himself. (see Eph.5:33/NIV)	i. For *He who loves his wife loves himself.* (see Eph.5:28/NIV) ii. After all, *no one ever hated his own body*, but he feeds and cares for it; iii. just *as Christ does the church—* for we are members of His body. (see Eph.5:29-30/NIV)
4. Leave your father and mother and be united to your wife. (see Eph.5:31/NIV)	And the two of *you will become one flesh.* (see Eph.5:31/NIV) This is a *profound mystery* about Christ and the church. (see Eph.5:31-32/NIV)

5.3 God Ordained Marriage

I. *God's way:*

God instituted the traditional marriage which is a *covenant between a man and a woman with God as witness.* (see Mal.2:12-15)

Examples of Traditional Marriages in the Bible...

1. God created the first man, *Adam* in His own image and gave him a *wife named Eve.* (see Gen.1:26-27; 2:22-24; 3:20)

2. God called *Abraham, the father of faith,* out of idolatry along with his *wife Sarah.* (see Gen.12:5)

3. God chose a beautiful *wife named Rebecca for Isaac.* (see Gen.24:67)

4. God called *Mary and her husband Joseph* to fulfill His will of being Jesus' parents. (see Matt.1:18-19)

5. *Zecharias and his wife, Elizabeth,* were parents to John, the Baptist, the forerunner of Jesus Christ. (see Lk.1:5; 57-60)

II. *Our Way Based on God's Way:*

As believers in Christ, we should follow God's way and marry only another believer in Christ, build a family unit and raise up godly children.

5.4 God Intends Your Life Partner To Be Your Helper

Lessons from the "First Marriage" ordained by God...

I. *God's Way:*

- *Adam was all alone and did not find a suitable companion...* When God created Adam, he was all alone in the Garden of Eden since he did not find a helper comparable to him *from amongst all of God's creation.* (see Gen.2:18-20)

- *God chose a female companion for Adam...*God said, "It is not good that man should be alone." So God decided to give Adam a suitable *female helper for companionship and intimacy to have godly offspring.* (see Gen.2:18; Mal.2:12-15)

- *God made Eve from Adam...*When God made Eve from out of Adam and brought her to him, Adam said: "This is now **bone of my bones and flesh of my flesh;** she shall be called Woman because she was taken out of Man." **God saw them as one flesh.** (see Gen.2:21-24)

II. *Our Way Based on God's Way:*

- *Thank God, You Have a Life Partner...* Think of the times when you were lonely in your life like Adam was, and now if God has blessed you with a partner, be thankful to God. If not, pray to God for a suitable partner.

- *Husband and Wife, One Flesh...*In a marital relationship, husband and wife should join together and become one flesh and love and care for each other. (see Gen.2:24)

- *Pride is the Cause for Strife...* Be faithful to your partner and enjoy your life together by treating each other well; for **only by pride comes contention.** (see Prov.13:10)

- *Mend Your Troubled Marriage...* If your marriage is in trouble because of attitude problems, you should work it out amicably with God's help. Divorce is not an option; for **God hates divorce.** (see Mal.2:16)

5.5 Simple Wedding Is God's Choice

I. *God's Way:*

- Scripture says that after making *the woman, God brought her to Adam* and gave her to be his wife. (see Gen.2:21-24)

- If God had desired to celebrate Adam and Eve's wedding with grandeur, He could have invited all of His heavenly hosts, the angels and He could have decorated the Garden of Eden and had an elaborate celebration.

- There was a reason for God to celebrate since it was the first wedding on earth, yet He chose to have a simple wedding for the first couple on earth.

II. *Our Way Based On God's Way:*

- You need not follow the ways of the world and imitate what people around you do.

- Don't be sad if you cannot have a grand wedding, as long as God is in it.

5.6 Servants & Masters—Remember, Your Master is in Heaven

COMMANDMENTS OF GOD FOR US TO OBEY	REWARDS FOR OBEDIENCE/ SUPPORTING SCRIPTURES
Servants...	*Be obedient as servants of Christ...*
1. *Be obedient* to those who are your masters according to the flesh, i. with fear and trembling, ii. in sincerity of heart, iii. *as to Christ;* iv. not with eye service, as men pleasers. (see Eph.6:5-6)	i. *doing the will of God* from the heart, ii. *with goodwill* doing service, iii. *as to the Lord,* iv. *and not to men.* (see Eph.6:6-7)
2. *Serve wholeheartedly,* as if you were serving the Lord, not men. (see Eph.6:7/NIV)	Because you know that the **Lord will reward everyone for whatever good they do,** whether they are slave or free. (see Eph.6:8/NIV)
Masters... 3. Treat your slaves as if you were serving the Lord, not men. 4. Do not threaten them. (see Eph.6:9/NIV)	i. Since you know that God who is both **their master and yours is in Heaven.** ii. There is **no favoritism with Him.** (see Eph.6:9/NIV)

6. Salvation, The Gift Of God & Not Of Your Works

COMMANDMENTS OF GOD FOR US TO OBEY	REWARDS FOR OBEDIENCE/ SUPPORTING SCRIPTURES
For the gentiles: By grace, you **be saved through faith,** and not of yourselves and not of works, lest you should boast.— Apostle Paul. (see Eph. 2:8-9)	1. For ***it is the gift of God.*** (see Eph. 2:8) 2. For God, who is **rich in mercy,** because of **His great love** with which He loved us, even when you *are dead in trespasses…* i. **He makes you alive together with Christ.** (see Eph.2:4-5) ii. He **raises you** up. (see Eph.2:6) iii. He makes you **sit together in the heavenly places** in Christ Jesus. (see Eph.2:6) 3. So that in the ages to come God might **show the exceeding riches of His grace** in His kindness toward us (believers) in Christ Jesus.— Apostle Paul (see Eph. 2:7)

7. Take Your Stand Against The Devil's Schemes

Put On The Whole Armor Of God

COMMANDMENTS OF GOD FOR US TO OBEY	REWARDS FOR OBEDIENCE/ SUPPORTING SCRIPTURES
1. Be strong in the Lord and in His mighty power. (see Eph.6:10/NIV) 2. Put on the whole armor of God. (see Eph.6:11)	So that you can take your stand against the devil's schemes. (see Eph.6:11/NIV)
What Is The Whole Armor Of God? 3. Stand firm … i. with the **belt of truth** buckled around your waist, ii. with the **breastplate of righteousness** in place, iii. and with your **feet** fitted with the readiness that comes from the **gospel of peace.** iv. Take up the **shield of faith**, with which you can extinguish all the flaming arrows of the evil one. v. Take the **helmet of salvation.** vi. Take the **sword of the Spirit,** which is the Word of God. (see Eph.6:14-17/NIV)	*Why Should We Put On The Whole Armor of God?* For our struggle is… i. not against flesh and blood, ii. but against the **rulers,** iii. against the **authorities,** iv. against the **powers of this dark world** v. and against the **spiritual forces of evil** in the heavenly realms. (see Eph.6:12/NIV)

COMMANDMENTS OF GOD FOR US TO OBEY	REWARDS FOR OBEDIENCE/ SUPPORTING SCRIPTURES
4. Take up the whole armor of God. (see Eph.6:13)	So that you may be able *to withstand in the evil day,* and having done all, to stand. (see Eph.6:13)
5. *Pray in the Spirit on all occasions* with all kinds of prayers and requests. (see Eph.6:18/NIV)	i. You, beloved, *build yourselves up* on your most holy faith, *praying in the Holy Spirit.* (see Jude 1:20) ii. For he who speaks in the Spirit, *speaks mysteries with God.* (see 1 Cor.14:2, 4)
6. Be alert and always *keep on praying* for all the saints. (see Eph.6:18/NIV)	For our struggle is not against flesh and blood but against the spiritual forces of evil. (see Eph.6:12/NIV)

7.1 Jesus Gives You Authority Over Satan

1. **Jesus has all authority...**Jesus proclaimed, "All authority has been given to Me in heaven and on earth. (see Matt.28:18)

2. **Jesus gives us, believers, the authority over Satan...** Jesus declared, 'Behold, I give you the authority over all the power of the enemy.' (see Lk.10:19)

3. *How do we use the authority over Satan?*

   - **Bind the strong man, Satan...**Jesus said, First bind the strong man and **then you plunder his house**. (see Matt.12:28-29)

   - "Assuredly, I say to you, **whatever you bind on earth will be bound** in heaven." (see Matt.18:18)

   - **Resist the devil...**Submit to God. Resist the devil and **he will flee** from you. (see James 4:7)

   - **Crush the mountains of Satan...**The Lord says, "Behold, I will make you into a new threshing sledge with sharp teeth; You shall thresh the mountains (of Satan) and beat *them* small, And make the hills like chaff." (see Is.41:15)

   - **Greater is He who is in you...**You can join with another believer and bind the devil; for He, the Holy Spirit, who is in you is greater than he, the devil, who is in the world. (see 1 Jn.4:4; Lk.10:19)

   - **Wait on the Lord** to be empowered by the Holy Spirit. (see Ps.27:14; Is.40:31)

4. *What are the ways to overcome Satan?*

   - By the Name of Jesus (see Matt.28:18; Phil.2:9; Eph.1:20-23)

   - By the Blood of Jesus (see Rev.12:11)

   - By the Word of our Testimony (see Rev.12:11)

   - By the Word of God (see Matt.4)

   - By the power of the Holy Spirit (see Matt.12:28; 1 Cor.6:19)

   - By fasting and fervent prayer (see Matt.17:21)

- By rejoicing and praising God (see Josh.6:20)

5. *Why should we bind Satan?*

   - Remember, Satan comes to steal, kill and destroy our souls; for he is the enemy of our souls. (see Jn.10:10)

   - Satan is a deceiver, who snares you into sin. So be watchful.

6. *Which evil spirits should we bind?*

Jesus said to those who believe in Him—In My Name, you shall cast out devils. (see Mark 16:17)

Following are some of the evil spirits which you should bind and cast out:

Spirit of Lust & Perversion	*Spirit of Fear*
Spirit of Pornography	*Spirit of Unbelief*
Spirit of Adultery	Spirit of Timidity
Spirit of Fornication	Spirit of Anxiety
Spirit of Prostitution	*Spirit of Depression*
Spirit of Murder	Spirit of Heaviness
Spirit of Anger	Spirit of Despair
Spirit of Violence	*Mind-blinding Spirit*
Spirit of Destruction	Spirit of Confusion
Spirit of Death	Spirit of Emptiness
Spirit of Unforgiveness	Spirit of Self-pity
Spirit of Bitterness	Negative Spirit
Spirit of Hatred	*Spirit of Suicide*
Spirit of Vengeance	*Spirit of Murmur*
Spirit of Envy	Spirit of Guilt
Jezebel Spirit	Spirit of Condemnation
Spirit of Pride	Spirit of Slothfulness
Spirit of Greed	Spirit of Stinginess
Spirit of Selfishness	*Spirit of Lies*
Judgmental Spirit	Spirit of Poverty
Spirit of Contempt	*Spirit of Theft*
Spirit of Strife	Spirit of Hypocrisy
Spirit of Discontent	*Spirit of Vanity*
	Spirit of Self-righteousness
	Spirit of Worldliness
	Spirit of Infirmity
	Deaf and Dumb Spirit

Spirit of Antichrist	*Religious Spirit*
Spirit of Blasphemy	Familiar Spirit
Spirit of Idolatry	Spirit of Divination
Spirit of Deception	Spirit of Sorcery
Spirit of Persecution	*Spirit of Witchcraft*
Spirit of Opposition	Spirit of Addiction
Dominating Spirit	*Spirit of Blindness*
Spirit of Rebellion	Legalistic Spirit
Tormenting Spirit	*Spirit of Division*
Devouring Spirit	*Spirit of Racism*
Accusing Spirit	
Spirit of Resistance	
Spirit of Disobedience	

Ref. Verses: Gal.5:19-21; Is.19:14; Prov.17:20; Matt.5:28; 1 Cor.6:9-10; Rom.1:26-28; 1 Jn.3:15; 1 Tim.6:9; Is.59:7; Ex.12:29; 2 Kings 19:35; 1 Jn.3:8; Matt.5:22; Ps.37:8-9; Matt.6:15; Heb.12:15; Rom.12:19; 1 Pet.2:1; Rev.2:20, 1 Kings 21:25; Prov.16:18-19; Prov.15:27; 1 Tim.6:10; Matt.7:1-2; Phil.2:3; 1 Tim.6:5-10; 2 Tim.1:7; Jn.3:18-19; Heb.3:16-19; Matt.6:34; Phil.4:6-7; Is.61:3; 2 Cor.4:4; 1 Cor.14:33; Ps.42:5; Ps.51:12; Ecc.7:17; Phil.2:14; Num.14:2; Rom.8:1; Prov.19:15; Prov.28:22; 1 Kings 22:22; Ps.40:17; Jn.10:10; Matt.23:23; Ecc.1:14; Is.64:6; James 4:4; 1 Jn.2:15; Lk. 13:11; Mk. 9:25; 1 Jn. 4:1-3; Matt.12:31-32; 1 Sam.15:23; 1 Tim.4:1; Rev.2:10; 1 Sam.16:14; 1 Pet.5:8; Rev.12:10; Rom.13:1-2; Eph.2:1-2; 2 Tim.3:5; Col.2:8; Lev.20:27; Acts 16:16; 2 Kings 21:6; 2 Chr.33:6; 2 Cor.4:4; Prov.20:1; Matt.16:6; 1 Cor.1:10; Prov.24:23

8. Walk Worthy Of Your Calling—Be One In Christ

COMMANDMENTS OF GOD FOR US TO OBEY	REWARDS FOR OBEDIENCE/ SUPPORTING SCRIPTURES
Be One in Christ...	*For there is...*
Walk worthy of the calling with which you were called...	*one Body* (Church) and *one Spirit* (Holy Spirit),
i. with all lowliness,	just as you were called in
ii. gentleness,,	*one hope of your calling;*
iii. with long suffering,	*one Lord,*
iv. *bearing with one another*	*one faith,*
in love,	*one baptism;*
v. endeavoring to *keep the unity* of the Spirit in the bond of peace. (see Eph.4:1-3)	*one God* and Father of all, who *is* above all, and through all, and in you all. (see Eph.4:4-6)

*Walk in unity...*To walk worthy of your calling and to be one in Christ, you should *be filled with the fruit of the Holy Spirit*, for e.g., lowliness, gentleness, long suffering, love etc.

9. You Are Made Alive In Christ! You, Who Were Dead In Your Sins

COMMANDMENTS OF GOD FOR US TO OBEY	REWARDS FOR OBEDIENCE/ SUPPORTING SCRIPTURES
1. Be made alive by trusting in Christ, you who are dead in your transgressions and sins. (see Eph.2:1; 1:12) 2. Do not walk according to the course of this world. (see Eph.2:2) 3. Do not walk according to the prince of the power of the air. (see Eph.2:2) 4. Do not be **sons of disobedience.** (see Eph.2:2) 5. Do not conduct yourselves in the lusts of your flesh. (see Eph.2:3) 6. Do not fulfill the **desires of the flesh** and **of the mind.**—Apostle Paul. (see Eph.2:3)	i. Or else you will be **children of wrath.** (see Eph.2:3) ii. For the **spirit of the prince of the air (Satan) works** in the sons of disobedience.—Apostle Paul. (see Eph.2:2)

Pause & Think!

- *Jesus Makes You Alive...*When you accept Christ as your Lord and Savior and develop an intimate relationship with Him daily, He keeps you alive in Him. (see Jn.10:10; Acts 17:28; Rom.6:11; Eph.2:5)

- *The Word of God Makes You Alive...*When you meditate on God's Word, His Word revives your soul and keeps you alive. (see Ps.19:7)

- *Obeying God's Commandments Makes You Alive...*Everyday as you wait on Him, Christ fills you with His Holy Spirit and helps you obey God's commandments to keep you alive. (see Matt.4:4)

- *The Holy Spirit Makes You Alive...*Know the power of the resurrection of Christ which can make alive every dead situation in your life including your marriage, your family and your sick body. (see Rom.8:11)

9.1 Jesus Accepts You Just As You Are

Know Who You Are In Christ & Declare It...

- You are *blessed* with *every spiritual blessing* in Christ. (see Eph.1:3)
- You have *citizenship in heaven*. (see Phil.3:20)
- You are *seated with Christ* in the heavenly realm. (see Eph.2:6)
- You are an *heir of God and joint heir with Christ*. (see Rom.8:17)
- You have an *inheritance* in heaven. (see Eph.1:11)
- You are *chosen* before the creation of the world *to be holy* and blameless in God's sight. (see Eph.1:4)
- You are *predestined* to be adopted as *children of God*. (see Eph.1:5)
- You are *adopted* as God's children *to live to His praise*. (see Eph.1:6)
- You are freely given God's *glorious grace* in Christ. (see Eph.1:6)
- You are *redeemed* through the precious blood of Christ. (see Eph.1:7)
- You are *forgiven* in Christ. (see Eph.1:7; Col.1:13-14)
- You are *justified* by faith in Christ. (see Rom.5:1)
- You are a *new creation* in Christ. (see 2 Cor.5:17)
- You are the *righteousness of God* in Christ. (see 2 Cor.5:21)
- You are *free from condemnation* in Christ Jesus, *when you walk according to the Spirit*. (see Rom.8:1-2; Gal.5:16)
- You are *made alive* in the Spirit. (see 1 Pet.3:18)
- You are *complete in Christ*. (see Col.2:10)
- You are the *temple of God*. (see 1 Cor.3:16)
- You have *direct access to the throne of grace*. (see Heb.4:14-16)
- You are not given the spirit of fear, but the *Spirit of power and love and a sound mind*. (see 2 Tim.1:17)
- You are *God's workmanship* created *for good works*. (see Eph.2:10)
- You *can do all things through Christ* who strengthens you. (see Phil.4:13)
- You are *delivered from the kingdom of darkness* and transferred into the Kingdom of God. (see Col.1:13)
- You are *rescued from the coming wrath of God*. (see 1 Thes.1:10)

Arise & Shine! You Are Precious In God's Eyes

10. You Are Equipped To Be Perfect In Christ

Jesus commands, *"Be perfect as your heavenly Father is perfect."* (see Matt.5:48/NIV)

COMMANDMENTS OF GOD FOR US TO OBEY	REWARDS FOR OBEDIENCE/ SUPPORTING SCRIPTURES
1. You should...	*Spiritual Gifts...*
i. *no longer be children,*	1. To each one of us *grace is given* according to the measure of Christ's gift. (see Eph.4:7)
ii. tossed to and fro	
iii. and *carried about with every wind of doctrine,*	2. For Christ Himself gave some to be *apostles,* some *prophets,* some *evangelists,* and some *pastors* and *teachers...*
iv. by the *trickery of men,*	
v. in the *cunning craftiness* of *deceitful plotting.* (see Eph.4:14)	i. for the *equipping* of the saints
2. No longer be a child but be a perfect man. (see Eph.4:13-14)	ii. for the *work of ministry,*
3. Speak the truth in love. (see Eph.4:15)	iii. for the *edifying* of the body of Christ,
	iv. till we all come to the *unity of the faith,*
	v. and of the *knowledge of the Son of God,*
	vi. to be a *perfect man,*
	vii. to the measure of the stature of the *fullness of Christ;* (see Eph.4:11-13)
	viii. *You will grow* to become in *every respect the mature body of Him* who is the head, that is, Christ. (see Eph.4:15/NIV)
	ix. *From Christ,* the whole body, joined and held together by every supporting ligament, *grows and builds itself up in love,* as each part does its work. (see Eph.4:16/NIV)

PART III

Commandments Of God From The Book Of Philippians

Book of Philippians

Paul, an apostle of Jesus Christ, wrote this epistle to the **Philippian believers** in the year A.D. 62/63 during his **prolonged imprisonment,** most likely in Rome.

The church in Philippi was established by Paul and his co-laborers, Silas, Timothy and Luke, during his **second missionary journey**. This was a generous church which supported Paul financially. (see Acts 16; Phil.4:15-16)

The main theme of this letter is *"Joy in living for Christ"* and it focuses on Christ Jesus as the purpose for living.

"Put it into practice—whatever you have learned or received or heard from me, or seen in me," says Apostle Paul. (see Phil. 4:9/NIV)

1. Be Worthy Of The Gospel When You Suffer For Christ

COMMANDMENTS OF GOD FOR US TO OBEY	REWARDS FOR OBEDIENCE/ CONSEQUENCES OF DISOBEDIENCE/ SUPPORTING SCRIPTURES
1. Whatever happens, conduct yourselves in a manner *worthy of the Gospel* of Christ.—Apostle Paul. (Phil. 1:27/NIV) 2. *Stand fast in one spirit*, with one mind striving together for the faith of the gospel.—Apostle Paul. (see Phil. 1:27) 3. Do *not be frightened* in any way by those who oppose you.—Apostle Paul. (see Phil. 1:28/NIV)	i. Then it is a sign to those who oppose you that *they will be destroyed*, but that *you will be saved—and that by God*. (see Phil. 1:28/NIV) ii. For it has been granted to you on behalf of Christ not only to believe on Him, but also to *suffer for Him*, as Apostle Paul did. (see Phil.1:29/NIV) iii. *He who has begun a good work in you will complete it* until the day of Jesus Christ.—Apostle Paul. (see Phil.1:6)

Points to Ponder...

- *If we suffer, we shall also reign with Him...*Be encouraged that in the end, the wicked will be destroyed in hell-fire and the righteous will be saved for eternity. (see 2 Tim.2:12)

- *Epaphroditus held in high esteem for his suffering for Christ...* Apostle Paul sent Epaphroditus, his fellow worker and fellow soldier in Christ, to the church of Philippi, requesting them to receive him in the Lord with all gladness, and *hold such men in esteem.*

- *For the work of Christ, Epaphroditus came close to death*, not regarding his life, to minister to Paul's need which the Philippian church failed to do for Paul. (see Phil.2:25-30)

2. Count All Things Loss To Gain Christ

COMMANDMENTS OF GOD FOR US TO OBEY	REWARDS FOR OBEDIENCE/ SUPPORTING SCRIPTURES
1. Whatever things that are gain to you, count these loss for Christ, as Apostle Paul did. (see Phil.3:7) 2. Count all things loss and rubbish, *for the excellence of the knowledge of Christ Jesus*, your Lord, as Apostle Paul did. (see Phil.3:8)	*So that...* i. You may **gain Christ** and be found in Him. (see Phil.3:8-9/NIV) ii. You may not have your own righteousness that comes from the law. (see Phil.3:9/NIV) iii. But you may have the *righteousness which is through faith in Christ*—the righteousness that comes from God on the basis of faith.—Apostle Paul. (see Phil.3:9/ NIV

Pause & Think...

What profit is it to a man *if he gains the whole world, and loses his own soul?* (see Matt.16:26)

3. Destruction For The Enemies Of The Cross Of Christ

COMMANDMENTS OF GOD FOR US TO OBEY	REWARDS FOR OBEDIENCE/ CONSEQUENCES OF DISOBEDIENCE
1. Do not live as enemies of the Cross of Christ.—Apostle Paul. (see Phil.3:18/NIV) 2. *"Join together in following my example,* brethren."—Apostle Paul. (see Phil.3:17/NIV)	i. For their *destiny is destruction.* ii. Their *god is their stomach.* iii. Their glory is in their shame. iv. Their *mind is set on earthly things.* (see Phil.3:19/NIV) v. But *our citizenship is in Heaven.*—Apostle Paul. (see Phil.3:20)

Pause & Think!

Apostle Paul states, "Imitate me, just as I also imitate Christ." (see 1 Cor.11:1)

Here, Apostle Paul asks us to follow his example because he never boasted about anything else but the cross of Christ. (see 1 Cor.11:1)

4. Eagerly Wait For The Savior, The Lord Jesus Christ

COMMANDMENTS OF GOD FOR US TO OBEY	REWARDS FOR OBEDIENCE/ SUPPORTING SCRIPTURES
1. Eagerly wait for the Savior, the Lord Jesus Christ. (see Phil.3:20)	i. For *our citizenship is in Heaven.* (see Phil.3:20)
	ii. For Lord Jesus Christ, by the power that enables Him to bring everything under His control, will *transform our lowly bodies* so that they will *be like His glorious body.* (see Phil.3:21/NIV)
2. Stand fast in the Lord. (see Phil.4:1) 3. Let your *gentleness* be known to all men. (see Phil .4:5)	For the Lord is at hand. (see Phil.4:5)

4.1 Lord Jesus Christ, The King Of Kings Is Coming Soon!

I. Two Events Of The Second Coming Of Christ

- Rapture or The Secret Coming of Christ
- The Visible Second Coming of Christ

Secret Coming of Christ—Rapture	Visible Second Coming of Christ
What is Rapture? 1. In Christian eschatology, the Rapture is a reference to *"being caught up"* (see 1 Thess.4:14-17) 2. The Rapture is *for the ready Church,* the Body of Christ. (see 1Thess.4-5; 1 Cor.15:50-54) 3. Only those who anticipate Christ's secret coming *will see Him* and will be taken up to Heaven. (see Rev 3:10; Mat 5:8; Heb. 9:28)	i. In the Second coming of Christ, *everyone, including those who pierced Him, will see Him.* (see Zech.12:10; Rev 1:7) ii. Jesus Christ will come down from Heaven *with His Saints after the tribulation period.* (see Zech. 14:5; Col. 3:4; Matt 24:29-31)

Where is the promise of His coming?

Apostle Peter says, "Scoffers will come in the last days, walking according to their own lusts, and saying, *"Where is the promise of His coming?*

For since the fathers fell asleep, *all things continue as they were from the beginning of creation."* (see 2 Pet.3:3-4)

But, beloved, *The Lord is not slack* concerning *His* promise, as some count slackness, but is *patient with you, not willing that any should perish* but that all should come to repentance. (see 2 Pet.3:9)

Be Warned!

II. *Purpose Of Christ's Coming*

Secret Coming of Christ—Rapture	*Visible Second Coming of Christ*
1. *To Rescue the Church from the Wrath of God...*The Rapture is to save the Church, the Body of Christ from the wrath of God which will be poured on the earth during the great tribulation of anti-christ. (see Luke 21:36; 1 Thess 1:10; 5:9; Rev 3:10)	1. Jesus comes for the Jews and Gentiles who are *redeemed* during tribulation. (see Zech 14:1-3) 2. Christ will *execute judgment* on all people. (see Rev. 19:11-21; Jude 1:14-15) 3. The Lord of lords will then *set up His 1000 year Millennial Kingdom* on earth. (see Rev. 20:4-6)
Satan cast down from Heaven to earth after Rapture... 2. *War will break out in Heaven.* Michael and his angels will fight with the dragon and his fallen angels. The heavenly hosts will prevail over satan and his fallen angels. (see Rev. 12:7-8) 3. *Satan,* the great dragon, who deceives the whole world, along with his fallen angels, will be *cast out of Heaven to the earth.* (Rev. 12:9) 4. *Woe to the inhabitants of the earth* and the sea! For Satan, the accuser of brethren, who *accuses us before our God day and night,* comes down to the earth, having *great wrath,* because he knows that he has a short time. (see Rev. 12:10-12) 5. Satan, in his fury, *sends the man of sin, the antichrist,* to torment people on the earth during the great tribulation period. (see 2 Thess. 2:3-12)	*Satan cast into the bottomless pit...* 4. Jesus sends His angel to cast the dragon, that serpent of old who is the Devil and Satan, into the bottomless pit, and shut him up, and set a seal on him so that he should *deceive the nations no more* till the 1000 years are finished. (see Rev 20:1-3)

6. **Believers who stand firm for Christ will overcome Satan** by the **blood of the Lamb**, and by the **word of their testimony**; and they will **not love their lives unto death.** (see Rev.12:10-11) 7. Please note that there are **4 theological opinions** about rapture: • Pre-Tribulation Rapture • Mid-Tribulation Rapture • Post-Tribulation Rapture • No rapture – only second coming of Christ	

III. *Supernatural Occurrences During Rapture & Second Coming Of Christ*

Secret Coming of Christ—Rapture	Visible Second Coming of Christ
Be Prepared To Meet The Lord Jesus In The Air... *Comfort one another with these words...* Apostle Paul says, by the Word of the Lord, that... **1. The Lord Himself will descend from heaven** with a shout, with the voice of an archangel, and with the **trumpet of God**. (see 1 Thess.4:14) 2. And the **dead in Christ will rise first.** (1 Thess.4:16)	*Jesus' feet on the earth...* 1. In that day, the Lord Jesus will come down to the earth and **His feet will stand on the Mount of Olives**, which faces Jerusalem on the east. (see Zech.14:4) 2. The *Mount of Olives shall be* **split in two,** from east to west. (see Zech.14:4) 3. **Jesus coming with His army, the Saints...**The Lord, our God will come on a white horse with all His saints, ***including those who are caught up in rapture.*** The saints will be clothed in fine linen, white and clean. (see Zech.14:5; Rev.19:14)

Secret Coming of Christ—Rapture	*Visible Second Coming of Christ*
3. Then we who are alive *and remain* shall be *caught up together* with them in the clouds to meet the Lord *in the air.* And thus we shall always be with the Lord. (see 1 Thess.4:17)	4. *Angels gather the elect...*He will send His angels with a great sound of a trumpet, and they will gather together His elect from the four winds, from one end of heaven to the other. (Matt.24:31)
4. Behold, I tell you a mystery: We shall *not all sleep,* but *we shall all be changed—in a moment,* in the twinkling of an eye, *at the last trumpet.* (1 Cor.15:50-53)	5. *Armegaddon War...*The Faithful and True God, the Righteous Judge will make war against the nations of the world in the Battle of Armegaddon. (see Rev.19:11, 15)
Then "Death is swallowed up in victory." (1 Cor.15:54)	6. *War against the Almighty God...* The King of kings, Jesus Christ, with a sharp sword that goes out of His mouth, smites the beast, the kings of the earth and their armies who will be gathered together *to make war against Him.* (see Rev.19:15,19)
	7. *Judgment on the Anti-christ...* The beast i.e., the anti-christ and the false prophet, who deceive the people on earth to receive the mark of the beast, will be taken and *cast alive into a lake of fire* burning with brimstone. (Rev 19:19-20; Jude 1:14,15)
	8. *Victorious Christ...*Thus the fierce wrath of Almighty God will be poured upon His enemies, the beast, the kings of the earth and their armies. (see Rev.19:15-21; Jude 1:14-15)

IV. Timing Of The Second Coming Of Christ

Secret Coming of Christ—Rapture	Visible Second Coming of Christ
The day and hour unknown…	*Is Jesus Your Savior or Your Judge?*
1. "That day and hour no one knows, not even the angels of heaven, but My Father only," says Jesus. (see Matt.24:36)	1. *As the lightning* comes from the east and flashes to the west, so also will the coming of the Son of Man be. (see Matt.24:27)
2. You be ready, for the Son of Man is coming at an hour you do not expect *as a thief in the night*. (see Matt.24:42-44)	2. Take heed to yourselves, lest your hearts be weighed down with carousing, drunkenness, and cares of this life and that Day come on you *unexpectedly*. (see Luke 21:34)
	3. For it will come *as a snare* on all those who dwell on the face of the whole earth.(see Luke 21:35)
Make sure you are not left behind… 3. Two *men* will be in the field: one will be taken and the other left. (see Matt.24:40) Two *women will be* grinding at the mill: one will be taken and the other left. (see Matt.24:41) 4. Watch therefore, for you do not know what hour your Lord is coming. (see Matt.24:42) 5. All the prophecies concerning the second coming of Christ are already fulfilled. So rapture can happen any day at any moment.	4. *Immediately after the tribulation of those days…* i. the sun will be darkened, ii. the moon will not give its light; iii. the stars will fall from heaven, iv. the powers of the heavens will be shaken. (see Matt.24:29) Then the sign of the Son of Man will appear in heaven. Then *all the tribes of the earth will mourn.* 5. They will *see the Son of Man* coming on the clouds of heaven *with power and great glory*. (see Matt.24:30)

V. Be Rapture Ready...Watch & Pray

Watch & Pray... Now that you know rapture is definitely going to happen, watch and pray and prepare yourselves and your loved ones to meet the Lord in the air. (see Matt.24:42)

Stand in the Gap... Since rapture is imminent, **cry out to God for the salvation of your unsaved** relatives, friends, neighbors, colleagues and people living in your streets, city and nation.

Salvation is the best gift you can give to your fellow human beings in these last days. Give them their **Messiah, Jesus Christ!**

Prophecies already fulfilled... All the prophecies concerning the second coming of Christ are already fulfilled. So rapture can happen any day at any moment.

Escape the great tribulation... Watch therefore, and pray always that you may be counted worthy to escape all these things that will come to pass during the great tribulation period of antichrist, and to stand before the Son of Man. (see Lk.21:36)

VI. Do Not Be Deceived By Antichrist, The Beast

- **Antichrist to be revealed soon...** The Day of the Lord, the visible Second Coming of Christ will not come until the antichrist, the **man of sin** is revealed first. (see 2 Thess.2:3)

- **World stage set for the Antichrist...** The mystery of lawlessness, the antichrist is already at work. (see 2 Thess.2:7)

- **Antichrist opposes God...** Antichrist, the **son of perdition**, will oppose and exalt himself above God. (see 2 Thess.2:4)

- **Antichrist sits in the Temple of God...** The **abomination of desolation**, the antichrist will sit as God in the third temple which is soon to be rebuilt in Israel. (see 2 Thess.2:4; Dan.9:27)

- *Antichrist calls himself "God"...*He will show himself that he is God. (see 2 Thess.2:4; Dan.9:27)

- *Satan empowers Antichrist...*The coming of the lawless one is according to the *working of Satan, with all power, signs, and lying wonders.* (see 2 Thess.2:9)

- *Perishing souls will be deceived...*The antichrist will come with *all unrighteous deception* among those who perish, because *they did not receive the love of the truth, that they might be saved.* (see 2 Thess.2:10)

- *Condemned for not receiving Jesus, the Truth...*For this reason God will send them *strong delusion* that they should *believe the lie of the antichrist* that they all may be condemned who did not believe the truth but *had pleasure in unrighteousness.* (2 Thess.2:11-12)

- *Judgment on the Antichrist, the Beast...*The Lord will consume the antichrist with the breath of His mouth and *destroy him* with the brightness of His coming. (see 2 Thess.2:8)

VII. *Do Not Receive The Mark Or The Name of the Beast Or The Number of His Name*

- *2000 Year Old Bible Prophecy:* "He causes all, both small and great, rich and poor, free and bond, to receive a mark in their *right hand, or in their foreheads*: (see Rev. 13:16)

- *No man might buy or sell, save he that had the mark,* or the name of the beast, or the number of his name." (see Rev. 13:17)

- *Fulfillment of Bible Prophecy:* Approximately 2000 years later, the microchip technology is available right now for this prophecy to be fulfilled in our generation. Be warned!

VIII. *Eternal Torment For Those Who Receive The Mark Of The Beast*

"If anyone worships the beast and his image, and receives his mark on his forehead or on his hand...(see Rev.14:9)

- He himself shall also **drink of the wine of the wrath of God,** which is poured out full strength into the cup of His indignation. (see Rev.14:10)
- He shall be **tormented with fire and brimstone** in the presence of the holy angels and in the presence of the Lamb of God, Jesus Christ. (see Rev.14:10)
- The **smoke of their torment ascends forever and ever.** (see Rev.14:11)
- They have **no rest day or night,** who worship the beast and his image, and whoever receives the mark of his name."(see Rev.14:11)

5. God Will Supply All Your Needs When You Help The Servants of God

COMMANDMENTS OF GOD FOR US TO OBEY	REWARDS FOR OBEDIENCE/ SUPPORTING SCRIPTURES
1. Share in the distress of the Servants of God, as the Philippian church did to Apostle Paul. (see Phil.4:14) 2. Share with the Servants of God concerning giving and receiving, as the Philippian church did to Apostle Paul. (see Phil.4:15)	*So that...* i. The *fruit will abound to your account.* (see Phil.4:17) ii. It will be *a sweet-smelling aroma, an acceptable sacrifice, well pleasing to God.* (see Phil.4:18) iii. *God shall supply all your need* according to His riches in glory by Christ Jesus.—Apostle Paul. (see Phil.4:19)

*Greet one another...*We should greet every saint in Christ Jesus as Apostle Paul exhorts the Philippian Church to do. (see Phil.4:21)

6. In Christ, You Are Circumcised In The Heart

COMMANDMENTS OF GOD FOR US TO OBEY	REWARDS FOR OBEDIENCE/ SUPPORTING SCRIPTURES
1. Watch out for the dogs, those evildoers, those mutilators of the flesh (circumcision). (see Phil. 3:2/NIV)	*Boast in Christ Jesus...*For we are the circumcision (of the heart) who serve God by His Spirit. (see Phil. 3:3/NIV)
2. Boast in Christ Jesus, as Apostle Paul did. (see Phil.3:3/NIV)	
3. Have no confidence in the flesh.—Apostle Paul. (see Phil 3:4)	

Points to Ponder...

- *Circumcised in the heart...*Apostle Paul states that we, gentile believers need not be circumcised in the flesh like the Jews, for we are circumcised in the heart as believers in Christ.

- Paul calls those who impose circumcision upon the gentile believers as *"dogs and mutilators of the flesh."*

- The Lord Jesus says that we should *not put heavy yoke* on people as the teachers of the law did.

- *Rejoice...*Paul exhorts us to rejoice, for in Christ we are set free from all the rituals and traditions (e.g., circumcision) imposed by religion. (see Phil.3:3)

7. Jesus—The Name Above Every Name

COMMANDMENTS OF GOD FOR US TO OBEY	REWARDS FOR OBEDIENCE/ SUPPORTING SCRIPTURES
1. *At the Name of Jesus...* *Every knee should bow* of those in heaven, and of those on earth, and of those under the earth. 2. Every tongue should confess that Jesus Christ is Lord, to the glory of God the Father. (see Phil.2:10-11)	i. For God has **highly exalted** Christ Jesus, and given Him the Name which is above every name. (see Phil.2:9) ii. Salvation is found in no one else, for there is **no other name under heaven but the Name of Jesus**, given among men by which we must be saved. (see Acts 4:12/NIV)

When you put Jesus Christ first in your life and obey His Commandments...

- *Blessings* of God will overtake you. (see Matt.6:33; Deut.28:2)

- *Goodness and mercy* of God will follow you all the days of your life. (see Ps.23:6)

- God's *favor* will surround you as a shield. (see Ps.5:12)

- Blessed are those who do His Commandments that they may have the right to the *tree of life*, and may enter through the gates into the city. (see Revelation 22:14)

7.1 The Awesome Name of Jesus!

I. Salvation In The Name of Jesus!

- *Salvation in Jesus' Name...* Salvation is found in no one else, for **there is no other name under heaven but the Name of Jesus given to mankind by which we must be saved**. (see Acts. 4:10,12/NIV)

- *Receive Forgiveness & the Gift of the Holy Spirit in Jesus' Name...* "Repent, and be baptized every one of you **in the Name of Jesus Christ** for the forgiveness of your sins. And you will receive the gift of the Holy Spirit," said Peter to the multitudes. (Acts 2:38/NIV)

II. Eternal Life In The Name of Jesus!

- **Eternal Life in Jesus' Name...**Many signs are written in the Scriptures so that you may believe that *Jesus is the Messiah*, the Son of God, and that by believing you may have *life in His Name*. (see Jn.20:30-31/NIV)

III. Power In The Name of Jesus!

- *Holy Spirit, the Helper sent by Father God in Jesus' Name...* "The Helper, the Holy Spirit, whom the Father will send in My Name, He will **teach you all things**, and bring to your remembrance all things that I said to you." (Jn.14:26)

- *Do Signs & Wonders in Jesus' Name...* Jesus declared, "These signs will follow those who believe:

- *In My Name...*

  they will cast out demons;

  they will speak with new tongues;

  they will take up serpents;

  and if they drink anything deadly, it will by no means hurt them; they will lay hands on the sick, and they will recover."(Mark 16:17-18)

- *Work Miracles in Jesus' Name...* John said to Jesus, "Teacher, we saw someone who does not follow us casting out demons in Your Name, and we forbade him because he does not follow us."

  But Jesus said, "Do not forbid him, for no one who **works a miracle in My Name** can soon afterward speak evil of Me. For he who is not against us is on our side. (Mark 9:38-40)

IV. Ask & Receive In The Name of Jesus!

- *Pray together in Jesus' Name...*"Where two or three are gathered together in My Name, **I am there in the midst** of them," promises the Lord Jesus Christ. (Matt.18:20)

- *Ask & Receive in Jesus' Name...*The Lord Jesus says to those who believe in Him, "Whatever you ask in My Name, that **I will do**, that the Father may be glorified in the Son. (Jn.14:13)

- *Ask Anything in Jesus' Name...*If you ask anything in My Name, **I will do it**. (Jn.14:14)

- *Ask the Father in Jesus' Name...*Jesus said to His disciples, "Most assuredly, I say to you, whatever you ask the Father in My Name **He will give you**." (Jn.16:23)

- *Ask in Jesus' Name & Receive that your Joy may be full...*"Until now you have asked nothing in My Name. Ask, and you will receive, that your joy may be full." (Jn.16:24)

V. Be Great In The Name of Jesus!

- *Receive a little Child in Jesus' Name...* Jesus said, "Whoever receives a little child in My Name **receives Me**; and whoever receives Me **receives Him who sent Me**. For he who is **least among you all will be great**." (see Luke 9:48)

VI. Do Good Deeds & Get Rewards In The Name of Jesus!

- *Bless the Children of God in Jesus' Name...*Jesus said, "Whoever gives you a cup of water to drink in My Name, because you belong to

Christ, assuredly, I say to you, *he will by no means lose his reward.*" (Mk.9:41)

- *Do Every Good Thing in Jesus' Name...*Whatever you do, in word or deed, do everything in the Name of the Lord Jesus, giving thanks to God the Father through Him. (Col. 3:17)

VII. *Surrender At The Name of Jesus!*

- *Every knee should bow at the Name of Jesus...*God exalted Jesus to the highest place and gave Him the Name that is above every name, that at the Name of Jesus every knee should bow, in heaven and on earth and under the earth, and every tongue confess that Jesus Christ is Lord, to the glory of God the Father. (see Phil.2:9-11/NIV)

Jesus' Name Truly Has Power!

8. Let The Mind Of Christ Be In You

If you have any encouragement from being *united with Christ,*
if any comfort from His love,
if any *fellowship with the Spirit,*
if any tenderness and compassion, *then you will have the mind of Christ,*
says Apostle Paul. (see Phil.2:1/NIV)

COMMANDMENTS OF GOD FOR US TO OBEY	REWARDS FOR OBEDIENCE/ SUPPORTING SCRIPTURES
To Receive the Mind of Christ...	*What is the Mind of Christ?*
1. Be like minded, have the same love and be one in spirit and purpose. (see Phil.2:2/NIV)	i. Jesus Christ, being in the **form of God**, did **not** consider it robbery to be **equal with God.** (see Phil.2:6)
2. Do nothing out of selfish ambition or vain conceit. (see Phil.2:3/NIV)	ii. But Christ made Himself of **no reputation.** (see Phil.2:7)
3. In humility, consider others better than yourselves. (see Phil.2:3/NIV)	iii. Christ took the form of a **bondservant.** (see Phil.2:7) iv. Christ came in the **likeness of men.** (see Phil.2:7)
4. Each of you should look, not only to your own interests but also to the interests of others. (see Phil.2:4/NIV)	v. Jesus **humbled** Himself, being found in appearance as a Man. (see Phil.2:8) vi. Jesus became **obedient to the point of death,** even the death of the cross. (see Phil.2:8)
5. Let this mind be in you which was also in Christ Jesus. (see Phil.2:5)	Therefore, God also has **highly exalted** Him and given Him the name which is above every name. (see Phil.2:9)

Points to Ponder... As God highly exalted Jesus Christ, you too will be exalted when you have the mind of Christ.

*Apostle Paul commends Timothy for having the mind of Christ...*Apostle Paul says that he found no one *like-minded* as Timothy who *sincerely cared for other believers.* For all seek their own, not the things which are of Christ Jesus. (see Phil.2:2-5, 19-23)

9. Let The Peace Of God Guard Your Hearts & Minds

COMMANDMENTS OF GOD FOR US TO OBEY	REWARDS FOR OBEDIENCE/ SUPPORTING SCRIPTURES
1. *Do not be anxious* about anything. (see Phil.4:6/NIV) 2. In everything, by *prayer* and petition, *with thanksgiving,* present your requests to God. (see Phil.4:6/NIV)	And the *peace of God*, which transcends all understanding will guard your hearts and your minds in Christ Jesus. (see Phil.4:7/NIV)
Fill your mind with good things... 3. Brothers, Whatever is *true,* Whatever is noble, Whatever is right, Whatever is *pure,* Whatever is lovely, Whatever is admirable, If anything is excellent or praiseworthy *Think about such things.* (Phil.4:8/NIV) 4. *Put it into practice*—whatever you have *learned, or received or heard from me, or seen in me,* says apostle Paul. (see Phil.4:9/NIV)	And the *God of Peace will be with you.* (see Phil.4:9/NIV)

10. Preach Christ Out Of Love & Defend The Gospel

COMMANDMENTS OF GOD FOR US TO OBEY	REWARDS FOR OBEDIENCE/ SUPPORTING SCRIPTURES
1. Do not preach Christ out of envy and rivalry but preach Christ out of goodwill. (see Phil.1:15/NIV) 2. Preach Christ out of love and defend the gospel, as Apostle Paul did. (see Phil.1:16/NIV) 3. Do not preach Christ out of selfish ambition but preach Christ sincerely. (see Phil.1:17/NIV)	The important thing is that in every way, whether from false motives or true, Christ is preached. (see Phil.1:18/NIV)

11. Press Towards The Call Of God In Christ

COMMANDMENTS OF GOD FOR US TO OBEY	REWARDS FOR OBEDIENCE/ SUPPORTING SCRIPTURES
1. **Press on** to take hold of that for which Christ Jesus took hold of you.—Apostle Paul. (see Phil.3:12/NIV) 2. **Forget those things which are behind** and reach forward to those things which are ahead.—Apostle Paul. (see Phil.3:13) 3. **Press toward the goal for the prize** of the upward call of God in Christ Jesus.—Apostle Paul. (see Phil.3:14) 4. Let us, **as many as are mature,** have this mind. (see Phil.3:15) 5. Let us walk by the same rule, let us be of the **same mind,** as Apostle Paul had. (see Phil.3:16)	*So that...* i. You may **know Christ**. (see Phil.3:10) ii. You may **know the power** of His resurrection. (see Phil.3:10) iii. You may **know the fellowship of His sufferings.** (see Phil.3:10) iv. You may **become like Him** in His death. (see Phil.3:10/NIV) v. You may attain to the **resurrection** from the dead.— Apostle Paul. (see Phil.3:11)
6. *"**Join together in following my example,** brethren."* — Apostle Paul. (see Phil.3:17/NIV) 7. "Keep your eyes on those who live as we do" says apostle Paul. (see Phil.3:17/NIV)	i. For many **live as enemies of the cross of Christ.** (see Phil.3:18/NIV) ii. For their **destiny is destruction.** (see Phil.3:19/NIV) iii. But **our citizenship is in Heaven.**—Apostle Paul. (see Phil.3:20)

12. Rejoice In The Lord, For Your Names Are In The Book Of Life!

COMMANDMENTS OF GOD FOR US TO OBEY	REWARDS FOR OBEDIENCE/ SUPPORTING SCRIPTURES
1. Rejoice in the Lord, my brethren. (see Phil. 3:1) 2. Rejoice in the Lord always. Again I say, rejoice.—Apostle Paul. (see Phil .4:4)	For the Lord is at hand. (see Phil .4:5)
3. "Rejoice" says Lord Jesus. (see Lk.10:20)	For *your names are written in Heaven*. (see Lk.10:20)
4. Let us be glad and rejoice and give Him glory. (see Rev.19:7)	For the *marriage of the Lamb* has come, and *His wife has made herself ready*. (see Rev.19:7)

12.1 Rejoice, You are Invited To The Marriage Of The Lamb!

- Scripture gives another reason for us to rejoice and be glad; for the marriage of the Lamb is at hand. And **"Blessed are they which are called *unto the marriage* supper of the Lamb."** (see Rev.19:6-9)

- *The righteous church, His Bride...*The church, His bride must be ready to be taken to Heaven in rapture to meet her Bridegroom, Jesus Christ.

- *Price to pay to be the Bride of Christ...*The bride should be arrayed in fine linen, clean and white; for the fine linen is the righteousness of saints. (see Rev.19:8)

- *Are you willing to pay the price to be the Bride?* Every believer is called to be the Bride of Christ. The bride should be pure, holy, righteous, without any blemish and delivered from all impurity.

- *Are you the Bride of Christ or the Guest at the marriage of the Lamb?* The Lord says that blessed are those who are called as guests at the marriage supper of the Lamb. (see Rev.19:9)

- How much more blessed will be the Bride of Jesus Christ at the marriage of the Lamb?

- *Reward...*To be the Bride of Christ is the most honorable reward a believer can receive in Heaven. (see Hos.2:19-20; 2 Cor.11:2)

13. Work Out Your Own Salvation With Fear & Trembling

Salvation is a free gift of God by grace through faith in Jesus Christ. But after you are saved, you are expected to work out your own Salvation by living your life in the reverential fear of God. (see Rom.10:9; Phil.2:12)

COMMANDMENTS OF GOD FOR US TO OBEY	REWARDS FOR OBEDIENCE/ SUPPORTING SCRIPTURES
1. Work out your own salvation with fear and trembling. (see Phil.2:12)	For it is *God who works in you* both to will and to do *for His good pleasure.*(see Phil.2:13)
How Do You Work Out Your Own Salvation? 2. Do all things without murmuring and disputing. (see Phil.2:14) 3. *Hold fast the Word of Life.* (see Phil.2:16)	i. So that you may become *blameless* and *pure,* "children of God *without fault* in a crooked and depraved generation." (see Phil.2:15) ii. For in the midst of a perverse generation, you *shine as lights in the world.* (see Phil.2:15)

13.1 Jesus, Tempted Just Like Us, Yet Without Sin

*Only those who endure till the end shall be saved...*Though Salvation is the free gift of God to mankind through Christ Jesus, Scripture says that only those who endure till the end shall be saved. (*Eternal Salvation*) Hence once you accept Jesus Christ as your Savior, for the rest of your life, you need to work out your own salvation by resisting sin with the help of the Holy Spirit. (see Matt.24:13; Rom.10:9-10; Phil.2:12; Jude 1:3; Heb.5:9; 9:28)

*You are being saved all your life...*For the message of the cross is foolishness to those who are perishing, but to us who are *being saved* it is the power of God. (1 Cor.1:18)

*Jesus, tempted just like us...*Jesus, when He walked on this earth in the flesh, was tempted in every way, just like we are, yet He did not sin. (see Heb.4:15)

Jesus learnt obedience through suffering, by denying His fleshly desires... Jesus, as a human being, went through suffering to resist all the temptations of the flesh in order to learn obedience. (see Heb.5:8)

*Jesus, our High Priest, empathizes with our weaknesses...*We do not have a high priest who is unable to empathize with our weaknesses, but we have one who has been tempted in every way, just as we are—yet he did not sin. (Heb. 4:14-15)

*Grace of God available to help us overcome sin...*Let us then approach God's throne of grace with confidence, so that we may receive mercy and find grace to help us in our time of need. (Heb. 4:16)

14. You Can Do All Things Through Christ Jesus

COMMANDMENTS OF GOD FOR US TO OBEY	REWARDS FOR OBEDIENCE
1. Be content whatever the circumstances, as Apostle Paul was. (see Phil.4:11/NIV)	For Christ *Jesus will strengthen you* as He strengthened Apostle Paul. (see Phil.4:13)
2. *Learn the secret of being content* in any and every situation, whether well fed or hungry, whether living in plenty or in want, as apostle Paul did. (see Phil.4:11-12/NIV)	
3. Do all things through Christ Jesus, as Apostle Paul did. (see Phil.4:13)	

Pause & Think!

- *Find out the secret...*Apostle Paul learnt the secret that he could do all things through Jesus Christ who strengthened him.

- *You can do whatever you are called to do...*Christ's power and grace enables us to do everything that He has called us to do and also to be content in every situation.

- Jesus Himself says, *"Without Me you can do nothing."* (see Jn.15:5)

14.1 You Can Do Greater Things Than What Jesus Did

*God molds your character before using you mightily....*When you are called by God to fulfill a greater purpose for His Kingdom, God will first take you through **His School of Training** to mold your character *into His image*. Your *"Ego. Self and I"* must die. It is a process and it depends on how quickly you yield to the Holy Spirit. The vessel has to be prepared so that he can do greater things than Jesus Himself.

*God trains you to Die to Self...*One of the ways to die to self is this—**God will put people with different attitudes in your path** to mold your character and to prepare you to do greater works for Him.

If you cannot **overcome the deeds of your flesh** like anger, pride, unforgiveness, bitterness, selfishness, lack of love, lust, etc., you cannot fulfill 100% of God's will for your life. God cannot use you mightily until you fully surrender to the leading of the Holy Spirit.

Total surrender to God = Pain of dying to Self + 100% Obedience to God

1. Ways to Die to Self

Some of the ways by which the Holy Spirit helps you crucify your flesh...

- *By Meditating "The Word"...*You should meditate on the Word of God *day and night* and the *Word of God will purify you.* (see Ps.1:2; Josh.1:8)

- *By Hearing Audio Bible...*You can hear the Word of God on Bible audio tapes and fill your mind with things of above thereby *renewing your mind.* (see Phil.4:8)

- *By Praying without ceasing...*You should come to the level of praying without ceasing. Then dying to self will be easy. (1 Thes.5:17)

- *By Praying in the Spirit 15-30 minutes daily...*You can pray in the gift of tongues at least for 15-30 minutes everyday which is the *shortcut to your calling.*

- *By the Anointing of the Holy Spirit...*You must daily wait on the Holy Spirit until He *cleanses your temple* for Him to dwell in and *strengthen your inner man* to overcome any temptation that the devil puts in your path.

- *By the Power of the Holy Spirit...*The Holy Spirit *removes the root of the lust of the flesh* from deep within your heart.—*Author's Experience*

2. Outward Signs of Dying to Self

*The prepared vessel bears the fruit of the Holy Spirit...*Once you are trained by God, you will have the fruit of the Holy Spirit and you will be able to *overcome your attitude problems, the lust of the flesh etc., which may hinder your calling.* Then you can handle any personality and adjust with any human being to achieve the greater vision that God has conceived in your heart.

3. Lessons to learn from the Biblical Characters...

I. Moses had to first "Die to Self" to become an Extra-ordinary Leader

*i. Moses, a Prepared Vessel...*Moses was prepared by the Lord for 80 years to deliver 2 million Israelites from slavery in Egypt. God molded his character and trained him for 40 years as a prince in the palace and 40 years in the wilderness as a shepherd. *It took Moses 80 years to die to Self, I, ego, etc.* (see Ex.2-3)

*ii. Moses lost his temper...*Moses became the meekest man on earth and yet when the Israelites provoked him in the wilderness and murmured against him for lack of water, he could not control his anger. Instead of speaking to the rock as the Lord had instructed him to bring water out of the rock, he struck the rock twice with his rod in anger. (see Num. 20:7-11)

iii. Moses' Disobedience prevented him from Fulfilling his Calling to the end... For whatever Moses did was symbolic of what was to happen in Christ's life. In the New Testament, the rock which Moses struck represents Jesus Christ, the spring of Living Water. (see 1 Cor.10:4)

Christ was to be Crucified only once for our Redemption, as Moses was commanded by God to strike the rock in the first instance of bringing water out of the rock. In the second incident, Moses struck the rock twice in anger when God had asked him to just speak to the rock. This is symbolic of Christ being crucified twice. Therefore God could not forgive Moses but punished him for his short temper and disobedience to God's command and did not let Moses lead the Israelites into the promised land, which was his ultimate calling. (see Ex.17:1-7; Num.20:1-13; Is.53)

iv. Moses' one act of Disobedience cost him Entry into the Promised Land... God's purpose in preparing Moses for 80 years was for him to lead the Israelites into the promised land. Sadly, Moses died in the desert without entering the promised land due to his disobedience. But God was so pleased with Moses' extra-ordinary leadership that God Himself buried him after his death. (Num.20:12; Deut.34:6)

v. Moses, an extra-ordinary leader, with whom God spoke face to face... Since Moses was prepared by God to die to self, God honored him as His chosen servant and revealed to him **every event that happened in the past, from the beginning of creation,** mentioned in the Book of Genesis, for example, how God Almighty created the heavens and the earth, how He formed man out of dust, how the first man Adam fell into sin, the redemption plan of God, etc.

It is amazing that God revealed to Moses not only the family line of Seth, the righteous son of Adam but also the family of Cain, the wicked son of Adam, who murdered his brother Abel. God also disclosed to Moses in detail the genealogy of Noah and the descendants of Noah's three sons, Shem, Ham and Japheth, after the flood destroyed the earth. Can you imagine God would make known to Moses **every small event that had happened in the lives of our forefathers, Abraham, Isaac, Jacob and Joseph?** Prophets of God have foretold only the future events but God revealed to Moses whatever had happened in the past, the events that took place even before his birth. How awesome it is that God would speak to Moses like this face to face!

II. Joseph, Purified by God's Word in the Prison

Joseph was another chosen vessel whom God prepared for 13 years before he was appointed second to Pharaoh of Egypt.

1. God's Way—Troubled Path But Victorious End!

i. Joseph, Enrolled in God's School of Training... God revealed to Joseph his calling through dreams when he was very young. (see Gen.37:5-11)

The Lord allowed him to be separated from his father Jacob, though he was his favorite son. God permitted Joseph to be thrown *into the pit* by his jealous brothers and then to be *sold as a slave* to work in Potiphar's house in Egypt. God's mighty hand was behind it all but God stopped Joseph's brothers from killing him. (see Gen.37:12-36; 39:1-6)

ii. Reverential Fear of God protected Joseph from Adultery... While Joseph was a slave in Potiphar's house, he was *tempted by Potiphar's wife* to commit adultery. Though Joseph ran away from the sin because of the great fear of God that was in him, *yet God allowed him to be put in the prison.* But God protected Joseph from being killed. (Gen.39:7-23)

God's favor was upon Joseph every step of the way. Even in the prison he found favor in the eyes of the jailer. (see Gen.39:20-23)

Though Joseph was righteous and ran away from the sin of adultery, yet *God did not rescue him from disgrace.* He had to endure the shame of being called an adulterer.

iii. Acting in the Flesh before God's Timing is Useless... In the prison Joseph interpreted the dreams of the Pharaoh's cupbearer and baker accurately. When the cupbearer was released as prophesied by Joseph, he requested the cupbearer to put in a good word to the Pharaoh about him. The Lord caused the cupbearer to forget about Joseph until it was God's timing to get Joseph out of prison, i.e., after 2 years. Joseph acted in the flesh but it did not work out for him *because the vessel was not fully prepared yet.* (see Gen.40-41) *iv. The Word of God Prepared Joseph in the Prison...* While Joseph was in the prison, they hurt his feet with fetters and he was laid in irons. Until the time that God's promises came to pass, the Word of the Lord tested Joseph, purified him and molded his character. (see Ps.105:18-19)

v. Intimacy with God through Prayer... Joseph must have developed a very close relationship with God during those two years he spent in prison that when Pharaoh sent for him, Joseph was ready to interpret his dreams. God had filled Joseph with so much of wisdom, knowledge and the gifts of the Holy Spirit that he not only interpreted the dreams but he also gave solutions to the problem and rescued the whole nation of Egypt from famine. (see Ps.105:16-22)

*vi. God honored Joseph's good attitude...*Joseph had all the reasons to murmur yet he **never murmured against God** even when he was in the prison. In due time, God lifted him up and made him second to the Pharaoh of Egypt. (see Gen.41:39-43)

In another instance, when Joseph had an opportunity to take revenge on his brothers who were the cause for all his problems, yet *he chose to forgive* them and also met all their needs during the times of famine. (see Gen.45)

2. Our Way Based on God's Way

i. Everyday we must wait on the Lord to be filled with the Presence and the Power of the Holy Spirit so that we can crucify our fleshly desires on the cross and die to "Self". Then God will be able to use us mightily.

ii. When you are half way through with God's training, you may feel like you are ready and you want to escape from the trials and the rest of the training like how Joseph acted in the flesh and anticipated his release from the prison with the help of Pharaoh's cupbearer before God's timing. But God will keep you in the same situation until you overcome your flesh and die to "Self". He will put you through the furnace of fire until your faith is purified as gold.

III. God Chased After Jonah, for He was a Prepared Vessel

i.God will not let go off a Prepared Vessel... Jonah was a prepared vessel of God. This is the reason why God chased him around and would not let go off Jonah when he ran away from God's calling. *God even used a great storm, a raging sea and a whale to make him repent* and be obedient to His will; *for a prepared vessel cannot turn back on God's calling.* (see Jonah 1-2; Lk.9:62)

ii. God taught the disappointed Jonah, His Ways... After being in the whale's belly for three days and three nights, finally Jonah obeyed God and prophesied the destruction of Nineveh.

When the people of Nineveh truly repented, *God chose not to destroy the city of Nineveh*. This angered Jonah. He showed a bad attitude because it affected his reputation as a prophet.

God had to teach Jonah His ways and make him understand *God's heart for lost souls* through an analogy of a tree. (see Jonah 2-4)

iii. *Jonah knew his God...*When God did not destroy Nineveh and did not bring Jonah's prophesy to pass, it displeased Jonah exceedingly and he was very angry and he said to God, "I know that You are a *gracious and merciful God, slow to anger and abundant in loving kindness, One who relents from doing harm.*" (see Jonah 4:1-2)

Do you know Your God like Jonah did? When you are in God's School of Training, God will be patient with you and work with your personality until He makes you into His image. He will teach you His ways.

IV. *Jesus gave up on the Pharisees, Though Teachers of God's Law, For They Resisted the Spirit of God*

i. Pharisees, Wise in their Own Eyes, missed Jesus, their Messiah... The Pharisees, the teachers of the Law, did not recognize their Messiah, Jesus Christ, who was in their midst.

*ii. Pharisees Crucified Jesus, their Messiah on the Cross...*The Pharisees were so *proud* of their knowledge of the Law that they refused to accept Jesus as the Son of God though Jesus repeatedly tried to convince them of his deity. They were the ones who eventually put Him to death on the cross. (see Jn. 11:45-53)

*iii. Pharisees Relied On Their Own Wisdom....*The Pharisees reasoned in their minds and *assumed that Jesus had come from the city of Nazareth* in Galilee while the Old Testament Scriptures clearly indicated that the Messiah would come from Bethlehem of Judah. *The Pharisees did not check out where Jesus was born nor did they enquire with His mother, Mary or His siblings.* (see Mic.5:2; Jn.7:41-42, 52; Mk.6:1-3)

iv. Jesus allowed the Pharisees to Perish in their Blindness... Jesus was born in the city of Bethlehem but *He did not reveal it to the Pharisees* because their attitude towards Him was not right. At one point Jesus even said to the Pharisees, "You are of your father the devil." (see Micah 5:2; Jn.8:12-47)

v. God had to let go off the Pharisees, the Teachers of God's Word, who were unyielding to His Spirit... On one occasion, when Jesus had cast out the demons by the Spirit of God, the Pharisees said that He cast out demons by Beelzebub, the prince of demons, thereby *committing the unpardonable sin of blasphemy of the Holy Spirit.* (see Matt.12:24-32; Lk.11:15)

vi. Eternal Damnation for willfully Rejecting the Messiah... On several occasions, Jesus tried to convince the Pharisees that He is the Son of God, He is the way to Heaven and He is the Bread of Life that came down from Heaven but they willfully rejected Him as their Savior and did not understand God's ways. Therefore, God allowed the Pharisees, the teachers of God's law, to die in their sin and go to hell. Jesus even rebuked the Pharisees by calling them, *"Serpents, brood of vipers! How can you escape the condemnation of hell?"* (see Matt.23)

vii. God let go off the Unyielding Pharisees but not Jonah, the Prepared Vessel... Though the Pharisees were the teachers of God's Word, God still had to let go off them because they were not yielding to His Spirit to *die to self.*

viii. Be Warned... Like the Pharisees, if we ignore the convictions of the Holy Spirit and harden our hearts to such an extent, then it is sad that God will be forced to give up on us too.

ix. Today, if you will hear His voice, do not harden your Hearts as in the rebellion... Scripture says, "Beware, brethren, lest there be in any of you *an evil heart of unbelief in departing from the living God*; but exhort one another daily, while it is called "Today," lest any of you be *hardened through the deceitfulness of sin.*" (see Heb.3:7-8, 12-13)

V. King David, Transformed Into A Man of Prayer During God's Training Process

i. David, Chosen to be a King, prepared by God for 13 years... At the age of 17, God anointed David, a little shepherd boy, to be the next king of Israel but first God had to take him through the process of preparation. (see 1 Sam.16:1-13)

*ii. David's Total Dependence on God...*For the next 13 years, as a part of God's training, David had to flee from King Saul who was after his life. It was difficult for David to hide in that small country of Israel and in the surrounding neighborhood. Many times he was just a foot away from death. During those perilous times David held on to God and *God was his only refuge.* (see 1 Sam.19-23)

David said, "The Lord is my rock and *my fortress* and *my deliverer; my God, my strength* in whom I will trust; my buckler and the horn of my salvation and my high tower. (see Ps.18)

*iii. David's Amazing Love for God...*During his flight from King Saul, David sang numerous *heart touching psalms* as no one else had ever sung before, expressing his love for God. (see Ps.18)

*iv. David, A Man of Prayer...*David talked to God all the time from the depth of his heart through his psalms. *David knew his God.* (see Ps. 3-7; 10; 13; 17; 20; 22; 25; 32; 51; 54; 60; 61)

David developed an intimate relationship with God during those 13 years of training before he became the king of Israel at age 30. *David fulfilled the will of God for his life in his generation.* (see Ps. 40:8; Acts 13:36)

*v. David's passion for God's Word...*We learn how to pray and talk to God through David's heartfelt psalms. He longed for God's Word with such passion that he repeatedly brings out in his psalms, the significance of God's Commandments, Statutes, Testimonies and the Law of the Lord. (Ps.19:7-14; 40:8)

VI. God's Chosen Vessel in the Furnace of Fire

*i. God is the Potter & We are the Clay...*The potter takes the clay and molds it into a beautiful clay pot but the process is not over yet. If the vessel is just sun-dried, it will break easily. So the potter has to put the vessel in the furnace of fire (900 degrees F). He then cools it and repeats this process over and over again several times till the clay pot becomes hardened to sustain the pressure. This process turns the ordinary clay into an exquisite piece of vessel ready for use, even in a royal palace. (see Jer.18:1-12)

*ii. Vessel taken through the Cave of Afflictions...*God takes us through the cave of afflictions, the furnace of fire, *to remove all the dross of 'self, ego and I'* from us until we are refined as pure gold ready for the Master's use just like how the potter molds the clay.

God knows that without the extreme heat of the fiery trials we will not be strong enough *to resist the crushing blows of Satan.*

God will not settle for 80% of yielding but will wait till the vessel is 100% ready for His use. We have to keep pressing on to fulfill 100% of God's will for our lives. (see Is.64:8)

PART IV

Commandments Of God From The Book Of Colossians

Book Of Colossians

Apostle Paul, while in prison for Christ, addressed this epistle to the *faithful believers* in Colosse in the year A.D.62. It is at times considered as a *"twin letter" with Ephesians,* because both epistles are similar in content and were written in the same year.

The Colossian church in Asia Minor may have been founded as a result of Paul's extraordinary three year ministry at Ephesus. (see Acts 20:31)

The main theme of this letter is the "Deity and Supremacy of Christ."

Special features... This letter strongly affirms *Christ's Divinity,* to oppose the dangerous false teachings in Colosse.

It emphasizes...

1. The truth of *Christ's Supremacy* in creation and redemption. (see Col.1:13-23)

2. That *Christ is the Son of God.* (see Col.2:9)

3. That Jesus is the *image of the invisible God.* (see Col.1:15)

4. That Jesus is the *fullness of the God head* in bodily form. (see Col. 2:9)

5. That Jesus is the *Creator of all things.* (see Col. 1:16-17)

6. That Jesus is the *Head of the Church.* (see Col. 1:18)

7. That Christ is the *all-sufficient One* for our salvation. (see Col. 1:14)

Apostle Paul says, *"Put it into practice*—whatever you have learned, or received or heard from me, or seen in me." (see Phil. 4:9/NIV)

1. Be Rooted & Built Up In Christ

COMMANDMENTS OF GOD FOR US TO OBEY	REWARDS FOR OBEDIENCE/ SUPPORTING SCRIPTURES
As you have received Christ Jesus, the Lord... i. so walk in Him, ii. *rooted* and *built up* in Him, iii. established in the *faith,* iv. and abounding in the Word with *thanksgiving.* (see Col.2:6-7)	i. So that you will be disciplined and *your faith in Christ will be firm*—Apostle Paul. (see Col.2:5/NIV) ii. Lest anyone should *deceive you with persuasive words.*—Apostle Paul. (see Col.2:4)

1.1 Jesus' Name Is "The Word of God"

Some interesting facts about the Bible, the Word of God...

- *Past, Present & Future of Mankind Revealed...*The Holy Bible is the only book which states the origin of the world, birth of man, his journey on earth and also the events that will happen in future.

- *The Universal Book...*The Holy Bible is universal and known around the world and there has never been a book written like it ever before.

- *A Historical Book...*The Holy Bible is written from actual human history. You can absolutely rely on it.

- *The Most Translated Book...*The Holy Bible is the only book in the world that has partially or totally been translated into more than about *1200 languages* and dialects. How amazing!

- *The First Printed Book...*The Holy Bible was printed in 1454 and it holds the honor of the first book to be printed.

- *The Holy Spirit Inspired Book...*The Holy Bible is written from 3 different continents—*Asia, Africa and Europe*, by *40 authors* inspired by the Holy Spirit of God.

- *The Most Sold Book...*The Holy Bible is the most sold book than any other book in the world; about *50 books are being sold every minute.*

- *The Most Shoplifted Book...*The Holy Bible is the most shoplifted book in the world.

- *The Most Read Book...*It is reported that the Holy Bible is the most read book among all the books in the world.

- *The Holy Book that offers protection to your children...* The Lord says that if you forget My Word, I will forget your children. (see Hosea 4:6)

- *The Only Life Changing & Life Giving Book...* God's Word is infallible, sacred, holy and true. It has been proven time and time again that millions of lives have been changed by the truth in the Word of God.

- *Don't you want to read this most popular Book called The Holy Bible?*

2. Be Not Deceived By The Tradition Of Men

COMMANDMENTS OF GOD FOR US TO OBEY	REWARDS FOR OBEDIENCE/ SUPPORTING SCRIPTURES
Beware lest anyone *cheat you through philosophy* and empty deceit...	i. For in Christ dwells *all the fullness of the Godhead* bodily. (see Col.2:9)
i. according to the tradition of men,	ii. *You are complete in Christ.* (see Col.2:10)
ii. according to the basic principles of the world,	iii. Christ is the *head of all principality* and power. (see Col.2:10)
iii. and not according to Christ. (see Col.2:8)	

3. Be Renewed In The Image Of Your Creator

Commandments concerning the following two topics covered in this Chapter will help you to be renewed in the image of your Creator:

- Put off the Old Man
- Put on the New Man

*Put off your old self...*If you live as you like, according to the worldly standard of righteousness, it will lead to *your spiritual death and eventually eternal damnation*; for Jesus says, *"Wide is the gate and broad is the road that leads to destruction, and many enter through it."* Hence you need to daily deny yourself of sinful pleasures of this world by the power of the Holy Spirit. (see Matt.7:13/NIV; Lk.9:23)

A true Christian cannot be comfortable in habitual sin because the Holy Spirit will convict him as soon as he commits sin. (see Jn.16:8)

*Put on your new self...*Jesus says, "Narrow is the gate and difficult is the way which leads to life, and there are few who find it." After you are born again, as a new believer in Christ, you should *walk in the narrow path of your Savior by obeying the commandments of God; for God's commandment is Eternal Life*. (see Matt.7:14; Jn.12:50)

If you were raised with Christ, then *seek those things which are above*, where Christ is, seated at the right hand of God. When Christ who is our life appears, *you also will appear with Him in* glory. (see Rom.6:4-11; 8:19; Col.3:1)

Set your mind on things above, not on things on the earth. For you died and now your life is hidden in Christ. Therefore, you must act like Jesus did by putting on the new man, manifesting all the 9 *"Fruit of the Holy Spirit."* (see Rom.6:4-11; Gal.5:22)

As a believer in Christ, *whatever you do in word or deed, do all in the name of the Lord Jesus*, giving thanks to God the Father through Him. (see Col.3:17)

3.1 Put Off The Old Man

COMMANDMENTS OF GOD FOR US TO OBEY	REWARDS FOR OBEDIENCE/ CONSEQUENCES OF DISOBEDIENCE/ SUPPORTING SCRIPTURES
Die to Self: 1. Put to death, whatever belongs to your earthly nature: Sexual immorality, Impurity, Lust, Evil desires and Greed, which is idolatry (see Col.3:5/NIV)	Because of these things the **wrath of God is coming upon the sons of disobedience,** in which you also once walked when you lived in them. (see Col.3:6-7)
Get Rid of the Sinful Nature: 2. You must rid yourselves of all such things as these… Anger, Rage, Malice, Slander and Filthy language from your lips. (see Col.3:8/NIV) 3. Do not lie to each other. (see Col.3:9/NIV)	i. Since you have taken off your old self with its practices. (see Col.3:9/NIV) ii. You have **put on the new self,** which is being renewed, in knowledge in the **image of its Creator.** (see Col.3:10/NIV)

3.2 Put On The New Man

COMMANDMENTS OF GOD FOR US TO OBEY	REWARDS FOR OBEDIENCE/ CONSEQUENCES OF DISOBEDIENCE/ SUPPORTING SCRIPTURES
Fruit of the Holy Spirit: 1. Clothe yourselves with… Compassion, Kindness, Humility, Gentleness and Patience. (see Col.3:12/NIV)	For you are God's chosen people, holy and dearly loved. (see Col.3:12/NIV)
Forgiveness: 2. *Bear* with each other and *forgive* whatever grievances you may have against one another. (Col.3:13/NIV) 3. Forgive as the Lord forgave you. (Col.3:13/NIV)	i. Even as Christ forgave you, so you also must do. (Col.3:13) ii. For if you do not forgive others their sins, your Father will not forgive your sins. (Matt.6:15/NIV)
Love: 4. Over all the above virtues, *put on love.* (see Col.3:14/NIV)	For love binds them all together in perfect unity. (see Col.3:14/NIV)
Peace of Christ: 5. Let the peace of Christ rule in your hearts and be thankful. (see Col.3:15/NIV)	Since as members of one body you were called to peace. (see Col.3:15/NIV)

COMMANDMENTS OF GOD FOR US TO OBEY	REWARDS FOR OBEDIENCE/ CONSEQUENCES OF DISOBEDIENCE/ SUPPORTING SCRIPTURES
The Word of Christ: 6. **Let the Word of Christ dwell in you richly...** i. As you teach and admonish one another with all wisdom. ii. As you sing psalms, hymns and spiritual songs with gratitude in your hearts to God. (see Col.3:16/NIV)	For you have put on the new self, which is **being renewed, in knowledge** in the image of its Creator. (see Col.3:10/NIV)

Your Words & Deeds:
 	
7. **Whatever you do...**
 	
  i. whether in word or deed,
  ii. do it all in the Name of the Lord Jesus,
  iii. giving thanks to God the Father through Him. (Col. 3:17/NIV)
	For you are God's chosen people, holy and dearly loved. (see Col.3:12/NIV)

"I will look on him who trembles at My Word"—GOD

- *Tremble at God's Word...*The Lord God Almighty states, "These are the ones I look on with favor: those who are humble and contrite in spirit, and who tremble at My Word." (see Is.66:2/NIV)

- **God's Word accomplishes His Purpose...**The Sovereign Lord declares, "So is My Word that goes out from My mouth: *It will not return to Me empty*, but will accomplish what I desire and achieve the purpose for which I sent it." (see Is.55:10-11/NIV)

4. Christ Is All And In All

COMMANDMENTS OF GOD FOR US TO OBEY	REWARDS FOR OBEDIENCE/ SUPPORTING SCRIPTURES
Put on the new self, which is being renewed in knowledge in the image of its Creator. (see Col.3:10/NIV)	*When you are renewed in the image of Christ*, then there is neither... i. Greek nor Jew, ii. circumcised nor uncircumcised iii. barbarian, Scythian, slave nor free iv. but **Christ is all and in all.** (see Col.3:11)

Points to Ponder...

- *Everyone is precious in God's eyes...*When you put on the new self, you are being renewed in the image of your Creator, Jesus Christ. Then you will see people as Christ sees them, for every human being is created in His image and Jesus Christ has bought every person with His most precious blood.

- *Abide in Christ...*Jesus says that if we abide in Him, He will abide in us. When Christ dwells in you, you are transformed into His image. (see Jn.15:5)

5. Do Not Let Anyone Disqualify You For The Prize

COMMANDMENTS OF GOD FOR US TO OBEY	CONSEQUENCES OF DISOBEDIENCE/ SUPPORTING SCRIPTURES
1. Do not let anyone who delights in false humility and the **worship of angels** disqualify you for the prize. (see Col.2:18/NIV)	i. For such a person who worships angels goes into great detail about what he has seen, and his **unspiritual mind puffs him up with idle notions.** (see Col.2:18/NIV)
	ii. For he has **lost connection with the Head,** (Christ) from whom the whole body, supported and held together by its ligaments and sinews, grows as God causes it to grow. (see Col.2:19/NIV)
2. Do not subject yourself to the regulations (ways) of the world. (see Col. 2:20/NIV)	i. For you have **died with Christ** to the **elemental spiritual forces** (fallen angels) of this world.
	ii. If you submit to the rules of the world, it is as though **you still belong to the world**. (see Col.2:20/NIV)
3. Do not submit to the rules of the world... **"Do not handle! Do not taste! Do not touch!"** which are based on merely **human commands and teachings.** (see Col. 2:21-22/NIV)	1. For these rules, which have to do with things that are **all destined to perish with use**, are based on merely human commands. (see Col. 2:22/NIV) 2. For such regulations indeed... i. have an **appearance of wisdom,** ii. with their **self-imposed worship,** iii. their false humility and iv. their **harsh treatment of the body,** v. but **they lack any value in restraining sensual indulgence.** (see Col. 2:23/NIV)

5.1 Satan Appears As Angel of Light

- *Worship of fallen angels...* The fallen angels that fell along with Satan when he rebelled against God, *can appear to human beings as gods.* Do not be deceived by these supernatural encounters of fallen angels. (1 Pet.3:19; Rev.12:9)

- Even Christians can be deceived *if they lose connection with the Head, Jesus* Christ.

- *Self Imposed Worship...* Apostle Paul also talks about rules concerning heathen worship, which appear wise and godly but they are merely teachings of men.

- *Rituals cannot buy forgiveness of sins...* The heathen religious leaders make people believe that they can please God by the harsh treatment of their bodies and they convince people that by following such rituals their sins will be forgiven.

- *No power to overcome sin...* The heathens practice only a "self-imposed religion" which does not give them any power to overcome the sins of the flesh. How sad!

6. God Reconciles You To Himself Through Christ

COMMANDMENTS OF GOD FOR US TO OBEY	REWARDS FOR OBEDIENCE/ SUPPORTING SCRIPTURES
1. Continue in the faith, grounded and steadfast. (see Col.1:23) 2. Do not move away from the hope of the gospel.—Apostle Paul. (see Col.1:23)	i. *Salvation*...You who once were *alienated* and *enemies in your mind* by wicked works, *Christ has reconciled to God,* in the body of His flesh through death. (see Col. 1:20-22)
	ii. *Perfection*...If you continue in the steadfast faith in Christ, then He will *present you holy, and blameless, and above reproach* in God's sight.—Apostle Paul. (see Col.1:22)

Pause & Think!

Salvation is the free gift of God but to be perfect in the eyes of God, you have to work out your own salvation with fear and trembling by obeying His Commandments. (see Phil.2:12-13)

7. Holiness In Family Life

COMMANDMENTS OF GOD FOR US TO OBEY	REWARDS FOR OBEDIENCE/ CONSEQUENCES OF DISOBEDIENCE/ SUPPORTING SCRIPTURES
Submission: 1. Wives, submit to your own husbands. (see Col.3:18) 2. Husbands, love your wives and do not be harsh with them. (see Col.3:19/NIV)	As is fitting in the Lord. (see Col.3:18)
3. Children, obey your parents in everything. (see Col.3:20)	For *this is well pleasing to the Lord.* (see Col.3:20)
4. Fathers, *do not provoke* your children. (see Col.3:21)	Lest they become *discouraged*. (see Col.3:21)
Prayer: 5. Devote yourselves to prayer, being watchful and thankful. (see Col.4:2/NIV)	Watch and pray that ye enter not into temptation. (see Matt. 26:41)

8. Holiness In Work Life

COMMANDMENTS OF GOD FOR US TO OBEY	REWARDS FOR OBEDIENCE/ CONSEQUENCES OF DISOBEDIENCE/ SUPPORTING SCRIPTURES
Employees... 1. Servants, obey your earthly masters in everything. (see Col.3:22/NIV) 2. Do it, *not only when their eye is on you* and to win their favor, but with sincerity of heart and reverence for the Lord. (see Col.3:22/NIV)	i. Whatever you do, work at it *with all your heart,* as working for the Lord, not for human masters, since you know that you will *receive an inheritance from the Lord as a reward.* (see Col.3:23-24/NIV) ii. It is the Lord *Christ you are serving.* (see Col.3:24/NIV) iii. Anyone who does *wrong will be repaid* for his wrong, and there is no favoritism with God. (see Col.3:25/NIV)
Employers... 3. Masters, provide your servants with what is *right and fair.* (see Col.4:1/NIV)	Because you know that you also have a Master in Heaven. (see Col.4:1/NIV)

9. Know The Mystery Of God, Christ Jesus

COMMANDMENTS OF GOD FOR US TO OBEY	REWARDS FOR OBEDIENCE/ CONSEQUENCES OF DISOBEDIENCE
Be encouraged in heart and united in love so that… i. You may have the *full riches of complete understanding*. ii. You may *know the mystery of God, namely, Christ*. iii. You may know Christ in whom are *hidden all the treasures of wisdom* and knowledge.—Apostle Paul. (see Col.2:2-3/NIV)	i. Lest anyone should *deceive you* with persuasive words. - Apostle Paul. (see Col.2:4) ii. For *God willed to make known* to His people among the gentiles, what are the riches of the *glory of this mystery, which is Christ in you*, the hope of glory. (see Col.1:27)

9.1 Supremacy Of Jesus Christ, The Son Of God

1. The Son of God, Jesus *Christ is the image of the invisible God*.

2. Jesus is the firstborn (*preeminent*) over all creation.

3. By Jesus Christ *all things were created:*

   i. things in heaven and on earth,

   ii. visible and invisible,

   iii. whether thrones or dominions or principalities or powers.

4. All things were *created through Jesus and for Jesus.*

5. Jesus Christ is before all things.

6. *In Christ, all things consist.*

7. *Jesus is the head* of the body, the church;

   Jesus is *the beginning;*

   Jesus is *the firstborn* from the dead;

   that in all things Jesus may have the preeminence.

8. For it pleased the Father that *in Christ all the fullness* should dwell.

9. By Christ, God *reconciled all things* to Himself.

10. By Jesus, God reconciled all things to Himself, whether things on earth or things in heaven, He made peace through Jesus' blood shed on the cross. (see Col.1:15-20)

10. Make the Most of Every Opportunity To Win The Lost Souls

COMMANDMENTS OF GOD FOR US TO OBEY	REWARDS FOR OBEDIENCE/ CONSEQUENCES OF DISOBEDIENCE
Believers... 1. *Pray* for the Servants of God.—Apostle Paul. (see Col.4:3/NIV)	i. So that God may **open a door** for the message of Christ. (see Col.4:3/NIV) ii. So that the Servants of God may **proclaim the mystery of Christ.** (see Col.4:3/NIV) iii. So that they may proclaim it **clearly,** as they should.—Apostle Paul. (see Col.4:4/NIV) iv. In order that whenever the servants of God speak, **words may be given** to them so that they will **fearlessly make known the mystery of the Gospel**, as they should—Apostle Paul. (see Eph.6:18-20/NIV)
2. Be wise in the way you act towards outsiders; **make the most of every opportunity.** (see Col.4:5/NIV)	i. Preach the Word; be prepared in season and out of season. (see 2 Tim.4:2/NIV) ii. He who wins souls *is* wise. (see Prov.11:30)
3. Let your **conversation** be always full of grace, seasoned with salt. (see Col.4:6/NIV)	So that you may know **how to answer everyone.** (see Col.4:6/NIV)
4. Take heed to the ministry which you have received in the Lord. (see Col.4:17)	That you may fulfill it. (see Col.4:17)

Preach the Gospel of Christ... The gospel of Christ is bearing fruit and growing throughout the whole world (see Col.1:6/NIV)

10.1 Bear Fruits For The Gospel Of Christ

- *Hear the Gospel of Christ...*The Colossian church believers heard the truth of the gospel.

- *Comprehend the Grace of God...*They truly understood the grace of God that Jesus Christ died on the cross in their place.

- *Have Hope of Eternal Life...*They comprehended the hope that is laid up for them in heaven through the Word of God.

- *Possess Steadfast Faith in Christ...*This revelation increased their faith in Christ and their love for all the saints.

- *Bear Fruits for the Kingdom of God...*Then they started bearing fruits for the gospel of Christ. (see Col.1:3-6)

- *Multiply Your Talents & Be Rewarded in Heaven...* As the Colossian church believers, when we truly understand what Jesus Christ has done for us on the cross and the hope that is stored up for us in heaven, we will also be motivated to bear fruits for the Kingdom of God and be rewarded accordingly in heaven. (see Matt.25:21)

11. Present Every Man Perfect In Christ

COMMANDMENTS OF GOD FOR US TO OBEY	REWARDS FOR OBEDIENCE/ SUPPORTING SCRIPTURES
1. Preach Christ. 2. Warn every man and 3. Teach every man in all wisdom, as Apostle Paul did. (see Col.1:28)	So that you may present every man perfect in Christ Jesus, as apostle Paul did. (see Col.1:28)

12. Set Your Hearts & Minds On Things Above

COMMANDMENTS OF GOD FOR US TO OBEY	REWARDS FOR OBEDIENCE/ SUPPORTING SCRIPTURES
Since you have been *raised with Christ...* 1. Set your *hearts on things above,* where Christ is, seated at the right hand of God. (see Col.3:1/NIV) 2. *Set your minds on things above,* not on earthly things. (see Col.3:2/NIV)	i. *For you died* and your life is now hidden with Christ in God. (see Col.3:3/NIV) ii. When *Christ, who is your life*, appears, then you also will *appear with Him in glory.* (see Col.3:4/NIV)

13. You Are Complete In Christ

COMMANDMENTS OF GOD FOR US TO OBEY	REWARDS FOR OBEDIENCE/ SUPPORTING SCRIPTURES
1. *Do not let anyone judge you...*	*For You Are Complete In Christ...*
i. by what you eat or drink,	*i. Circumcised by Christ...*In Christ, you are circumcised by putting off the sinful nature; not with the circumcision done by the hands of men but with the circumcision done by Christ. (see Col.2:10-11)
ii. or with regard to a religious festival,	
iii. or a New Moon celebration,	
iv. or a Sabbath day. (see Col. 2:16/NIV)	
	*ii. Buried with Christ...*You are buried with Him in baptism. (see Col.2:12)
These are a shadow of the things that were to come; *the reality, however, is found in Christ.* (see Col.2:17/NIV)	*iii. Raised with Christ...*You are raised with Him through your faith in the power of God, who raised Christ from the dead. (see Col.2:12)
2. Do not let anyone who delights in false humility and the *worship of angels disqualify you.* (see Col.2:18/NIV)	
	*iv. Alive with Christ...*When you were dead in your sins and in the uncircumcision of your sinful nature, God made you alive with Christ. (see Col.2:13)

COMMANDMENTS OF GOD FOR US TO OBEY	REWARDS FOR OBEDIENCE/ SUPPORTING SCRIPTURES

1. *Do not let anyone judge you...*
 	
  i. by what you eat or drink,
  ii. or with regard to a religious festival,
  iii. or a New Moon celebration,
  iv. or a Sabbath day. (see Col. 2:16/NIV)
 	
These are a shadow of the things that were to come; *the reality, however, is found in Christ.* (see Col.2:17/NIV)
 	
2. Do not let anyone who delights in false humility and the *worship of angels disqualify you.* (see Col.2:18/NIV)
	For You Are Complete In Christ...
	
	*v. Forgiven by Christ...*He forgave us all our sins, having **cancelled the written code** with its regulations that was against us, and that stood opposed to us; he took it away, **nailing it to the Cross.** (see Col.2:14/NIV)
	
	vi. Christ Disarmed Principalities & Powers of Darkness...
	Having disarmed the powers and authorities, Christ made a public spectacle of them. (see Col.2:15/NIV)
	
	*vii. Christ Triumphed over the Powers of Darkness for you...*Christ Jesus triumphed over the powers and authorities **by the Cross.** (see Col.2:15/NIV)

*Jesus Christ is the True God and Eternal Life...*The reality is found in Christ and since *you are complete in the Lord Jesus Christ*, you don't need to worship any other deity or angels but Christ alone. (see 1 Jn.5:20)

"If You Love Me, Keep My Commandments"–Jesus Christ

- Jesus says, *"If you love Me, keep My Commandments." (Jn. 14:15)*

- "He who has My Commandments and keeps them, *it is he who loves Me."* (Jn.14:21)

- *Whoever despises the Word brings destruction on himself,* but *he who reveres the Commandment will be rewarded.* (Prov.13:13)

- *Blessed* are those who *do His Commandments* that they may have the right to the *tree of life*, and may *enter through the gates* into the city. (see Rev.22:14)

COMMANDMENTS OF GOD FOR US TO OBEY	REWARDS FOR OBEDIENCE/ CONSEQUENCES OF DISOBEDIENCE/ SUPPORTING SCRIPTURES
Duty of all Mankind: 1. Fear God and keep His commandments. (Ecc.12:13)	i. For this is the *duty of all mankind*. ii. For God will bring every deed into *judgment*, including every hidden thing, whether it is good or evil. (Ecc.12:13-14/NIV)
Blessings for you & your children forever: 2. Observe and **obey** all these words which I command you - Lord God Almighty. (see Deut.12:28)	That it may *go well with you and your children after you forever*, when you do what is good and right in the sight of the LORD your God. (see Deut.12:28)
Abide in Jesus' Love: 3. Keep My Commandments just as I have kept My Father's commandments and abide in His love.—Jesus (see Jn.15:10)	Then you will abide in My love, says Jesus. (see Jn.15:10)
You are Blessed: 4. Hear the Word of God and **keep it**. (see Lk.11:28)	Those who hear the Word of God and keep it are **blessed**. (see Lk.11:28)

COMMANDMENTS OF GOD FOR US TO OBEY	REWARDS FOR OBEDIENCE/ CONSEQUENCES OF DISOBEDIENCE/ SUPPORTING SCRIPTURES
Prosperity & Good Success: 5. This Book of the Law shall not depart from your mouth, but you shall meditate in it day and night. 6. ***Observe to do*** according to all that is written in the Law. (see Josh.1:8)	For then you will make your way ***prosperous***, and then you will have ***good success***. (see Josh.1:8)
Be Righteous in God's sight: 7. Hear and obey the Law. (see Rom.2:13)	For it is not those who hear the law who are righteous in God's sight, but it is those who obey the law who will be declared righteous. (see Rom.2:13/NIV)

Peace to the brothers and sisters,

Love with faith from God the Father
and the Lord Jesus Christ.

Grace to all who love our Lord Jesus Christ
with an undying love. (Eph.6:23-24)

"If you love Me, keep My Commandments."—Jesus
(Jn.14:15)

About The Author

TESTIMONY OF DR. ESTHER V. SHEKHER

Greetings in His Most Holy Name from Christ Rules Ministries!

Salvation Experience...I accepted Christ as my Lord and Savior at the age of 18. During the course of my salvation experience, two facts became crystal clear to me -

- *Jesus loved me so deeply that He would even die for me.*
- *He hated sin so much that He would bear the suffering and shame of the cross to deliver me from that awful sin.*

I understood at that early age that I too must hate sin and I started longing for His righteousness. After yearning for the anointing of the Holy Spirit for a year, God baptized me with His Spirit for about 3 hours.

Promise of God Fulfilled...Jesus Christ became my passion and I spent a lot of time talking to Him daily. Jesus became my best friend. While I was doing my medical training, one day, after crying out to the Lord for about six hours, longing to see Him, to hear His voice and to know His will for my life, the Lord promised me through the Scriptures *(Acts 22:14) that I would see the Just One, hear Him speak and know His will.* This promise came to pass seven years later; for Jesus says, "My sheep will hear My voice."

Calling of God...I started spending 3-4 hours every day in fervent prayer and the Word. On March 18, 1992, while I was pouring my heart to God in prayer, I heard His ***audible voice*** saying, ***"I died on the cross for you, what have you done for Me?*** Will you do my ministry until you have your last breath?" From then on, I heard Him almost every night, waking me up at 3 a.m. saying, ***"Stand in the gap and cry out in the middle of the night with agony for the perishing souls."*** I have been obeying the Lord as He instructs me every single day. Our God is faithful in fulfilling His promises.

God molded my character over a period of several years by taking me through numerous trials, cave of afflictions. He trained me to die to self and to depend on Him instead of my own abilities. His awesome Presence, *His precious Holy Spirit, like a ball of fire cleanses the temple of my spirit everyday* and fills me, preparing me for His Ministry.

The Lord, in His grace, enrolled me in His School of Training. He prepared me by taking me through various trials, especially *the four major tests, namely, Character Test, Obedience Test, Word Test and Faith Test*, for the next 14 years. The tests got tougher and tougher and finally, to be honest before God, I felt like I was taking Ph.D. level exams in these four spiritual areas. Only by the grace of God, I could pass these tests according to God's standard of righteousness. All glory be to God!

Ministry Highlights:

Mission Trip...God called me as a full time Missionary and Evangelist in 2003. I obeyed His call and since then, I have been preaching the Gospel of Jesus Christ in many nations around the world, for the past 12 years.

Preaching Ministry...The Lord said to me, after preparing me for His calling for many years, *"Now you are worthy to preach to the Pastors and Believers of nations around the world."* The Lord Himself opened up opportunities for me to speak in Pastors' Conferences. I ended up speaking in about 35 Pastors' Conferences across Asia.

I have also spoken in numerous Churches of all denominations, Bible College, Prayer Revival Conferences, Women's Meetings, Youth Camps, Rural Outreach, etc., strengthening the believers and winning the lost to Christ. Praise be to God!

Set up "Christ Rules Ministries"...The Lord enabled me to establish "Christ Rules Ministries" in 2008, to raise up fervent Intercessors and worthy Laborers for the Kingdom of God, to win the perishing souls to Christ.

Established International Prayer Network (IPN)...The Lord gave me a divine strategy to start prayer cells through International Prayer Network (IPN) which I established in 2010, to *intercede for the Salvation of every lost soul in America* and other nations of the world. I have successfully implemented this IPN Prayer Strategy in USA, Sri Lanka, Malaysia, Singapore, India, Andamans, etc. By God's grace, with the help of the Pastors and believers, more than 7000 Prayer Cells have been started so far in these nations. Praise be to our God!

Prayer Ministry in USA... Since 2012, I have been preaching in several Churches in Stockton, Hayward, Galt and Bay Area in Northern California, and in Georgia, USA. I have sowed the seed of prayer in the hearts of people, encouraging believers to intercede for the Salvation of every perishing soul living in these cities.

Publications...By God's grace, I have written 2 books entitled, *"All the Commandments of God"* Volume I & II, which are published in USA. Jesus says, "If you love Me, obey My Commandments." The first book is a *checklist of Jesus' commandments* with their rewards and consequences clearly explained, from the Gospels of Matthew and John, covering all the major topics in Christian faith. This second book is also on the same concept of God's Commandments, taken from the Epistles of Apostle Paul.

TV Ministry... By the grace of God, I started the TV Ministry in 2011 to preach on End Times, the Commandments of God, the God given strategy to start prayer cells in various nations and to prepare the churches to meet our Bridegroom, Jesus Christ in Rapture.

Presently, God has been opening TV interviews across America, based on my books. Praise be to our God!

Seminars on End Times...I have also been preaching on End Times and teaching the whole *"Book of Revelation"* using powerful power-point presentations, to bring the awareness about the Second Coming of Jesus Christ, in various Churches.

Social work...Started Gypsy Literacy Programs, Widows Ministry, Handicapped Ministry, Orphanage Ministry, etc., in Asia.

All the promises that the Lord has given me so far are coming to pass one by one. I humbly yield myself to the Master, to be used for His glory.

My desire is to fulfill His will each and every day of my life. Blessed be His Holy Name!

MINISTRY MOTTO: PRAY, GIVE, GO OR
SEND FOR THE KINGDOM OF GOD

CHRIST RULES OFFICES

To Contact the Author, Write/Call:

In USA
Dr. Esther V. Shekher
P O Box 994
Galt, CA 95632, USA
Dr. Esther +1 (626) 450—5973
Michelle +1 (480) 251—1979
Darla +1 (209) 401—1696
Vincent +1 (626) 430—6674
Email: christrulesnations@gmail.com/christrules@hotmail.co.uk
Website: www.christrulesnations.org
Facebook: Christ Rules Nations

If this book has blessed you, please do write your
testimony and/or prayer requests.

In Singapore
Call Ms. Maya +65 98277554

In Malaysia
Contact: Pr. Nathaneal
E-07-12, PPR Muhibbah,
Jalan 15/155 of Jalan Puchong Taman,
Taman Muhibbah 58200, Kuala Lumpur, Malaysia.
Cell No. +60173204571

In India
H/3E, Sunshine Apartments
West Jones Road, West Saidapet,
Chennai 600 015, Tamil Nadu, India.
Call +91-9994709461/9791198673

Printed in the United States
By Bookmasters